RUNNING BAREFOOT
— *through the* —
SOUTHERN PIEDMONT

BUDDY BOWMAN

Copyright © 2023 by Buddy Bowman

Running barefoot through the Southern Piedmont

All rights reserved.

No part of this publication may be reproduced or transmitted in any form or by any means electronic or mechanical, including photocopy, recording, or any information storage and retrieval system now known or invented, without permission in writing from the publisher, except by a reviewer who wishes to quote brief passages in connection with a review written for inclusion in a magazine, newspaper, or broadcast.

Print ISBN: 979-8-35090-268-6

Printed in the United States of America

TABLE OF CONTENTS

Preface I	1
The Beginning of a Journey	6
Joanna	11
Around the Loop	14
A Year in Time Out	18
Main Street, Cross Hill	27
The Downs and Ups of a Mid-Century	39
Ed Leaman	44
I'll Always Be a Victor Boy	47
Little Old Greer's Post 115 Goes National	70
Scouting Adventures with Tom Wilson	77
The Gypsy Carnival	87
The Magic of Movies	89
Puberty Was Not a Picnic	94
A Flirtation with Juvenile Delinquency	103
Speed Traps and Other Surprises	107
Tales of a Barefoot Runner	111
The Tracks We Left, Crossed and Followed	116
Memories of Old Greer High	125
The Ralph Voyles Way	150
The Knothole Club	154
Bootleg Whiskey, Hot Rods and Music	159
Annie, an Inconspicuous Star	168
The Unforgettable, Uncompromising, Creative, and Adventurous Bill Groce	171
The Nearly Lost Art of Hitchhiking	184
What I Left Behind	189

DEDICATION

In memory of my childhood friend Ed Leaman, who always loved a good story, and to my friend and colleague at Gainesville High, Michele Breeden. Both left us too soon.

To Maya, who has always been there through dark and happy moments, and those in between.

ACKNOWLEDGEMENTS

A special orchid for Leland Burch and Walter Burch for including some of my articles about growing up in Greer in a column entitled *Up on the Mill Hill*. It gave me an opportunity to share with friends, in Greer, some special memories, as they were published in *The Greer Citizen*.

Thanks to Theresa Merck for scanning old pictures, and giving me lessons in computer savvy along the way. My appreciation to Laveda Miles, of Rochester, N.Y., formerly of Henderson Advertising, for enlightening me on the legal aspects of writing, for her reads on articles I've written, and for combining my stories into a manuscript, a mammoth task, in itself.

Gratefulness to Doug Wilson, Tom Wilson's son, and Mack Allen, both of whom have shown astute accuracy in the recall of details. They both were called upon more than once, to verify facts. I'm blessed to have Judy Gravley and Linda Bruce Terry for steady encouragement and sharing of memories, some of which are included within.

To the late Lois Austin, my main link to the past in and around Cross Hill. Our visits and talks were invaluable. You are missed, dear lady.

To my old dog, Buck, who was with me for 15½ years, for roads travelled and our conversations along the way. I couldn't have asked for a better companion.

To my primary M.D., Tom Murray, who has kept me patched up and healthy enough to finish this book.

To my wife Rebecca Shockley Bowman, for her patience and support throughout the writing of this book. She made many sacrifices.

To Dee Clayton and Jan Cox, the best critics a man could ask for.

Michael V. Clayton, copy editor of Time/Life, retired, was with me, from the beginning, with articles written for the *Greer Citizen*. He edited this book, as well, and has always been a friend during the greatest time of need. A wonderful friendship was born when we ran track together at Greer High, and still continues today, as he jogs by the Hudson.

PREFACE

I

This is a book about and for kids, a book with heroes and heroines who, like angels, descend upon us in moments of need. And by "kids", I mean the kind Frank Sinatra sang about, everyone who is still young at heart, which includes me and, I suspect, many of you.

It is also about a journey, as seen through the eyes of a son, a brother, and a young man, me actually, who experienced a trek with his family during a time of great social and economic transition, the beginning of the end of the textile industry, as we knew it, in the southeastern region of the United States.

It was a time when we rejoiced in the simpler things, like sitting around the table as a family, for meals, or listening to favorite programs on the radio, or learning the hardship of unexpected tragedies, through which we supported one another through our deeds.

Friendships are made throughout our life's journey, but a unique bond was created and existed among those, both male and female, who resided in mill villages and among other small communities, especially with athletes who competed in the various sports sponsored by the owners of mills in upstate South Carolina in and around the city of Greenville, which had the largest population of textile mill workers.

The same plan for community development was used in many of the villages built by owners of textile mills in the southeast but each had its own identity and demonstrated pride in achievements and in where they lived. Like many, I consider all inhabitants of mill villages to be brothers and sisters. Even though many of the mills no longer exist, out of the rubble memories remain.

Each community in which I resided had people who made lasting impressions. Heroes and heroines existed in some and came in a variety of forms, even the four-legged kind.

Finally, my family's experiences, through short stays in several locations, some rural, others larger and somewhat more progressive, allowed an adventurous lifestyle and a chance for our love to grow for one another. Old friends were left behind, though never forgotten, but we could always look to family for support, and it brought us closer.

I treasure the time spent growing up with my family and friends in my journey.

II

Who and where are our Heroes and Heroines?

Merriam-Webster's Dictionary defines the term *hero* as "an illustrious warrior admired for achievements and noble qualities who shows great courage." It also defines a *heroine* as "a woman with the same qualities of a hero."

As time has passed, we've personalized the meaning of the term. We each would have our own definitions of heroes and heroines.

Perhaps we should broaden the definition to include not just those known for bravery in danger or deeds on the battlefield, even though we're thankful for what they've done for our country, and we believe them to be deserving of any honor bestowed upon them, but also those who enter or exist in our lives during crucial times and affect us in a positive manner. In that sense, we do personalize them. Each of us have our own heroes and heroines who will never receive personal recognition, but are so important in our lives.

Sometimes they are all around us and we don't realize it until our races have all been run, our mountains climbed, and we're on the horizon peering back, at the end of our lives, contemplating the questions: What have I done with my life? Who and what was important? What made those important people so special?

What could we have done without family, who've made tremendous sacrifices and demonstrated through love and deeds ways to make our lives better? How about those who, with a smile, were gifted with the patience to handle small, noisy kids? The teacher who instilled the love of reading when she ended the day after having read a chapter from the Hardy Boys, by saying, as she arrived at a very interesting part, "And we will continue there tomorrow."

The coach who went the distance in refusing to let you quit, inculcating the values that would eventually become yours or the friend who was there to rejoice precious moments but also came to your rescue during life's low points. Even the animal who watched patiently with great anticipation for the moment when you entered the door, living to be with his master, serving him, sometimes by giving up his life. How about the religious leader whose deeds matched his words of wisdom as he was always active in our lives?

We all have our own personal heroes and heroines, and it is hard to imagine where we would have been without them. Mine were very special and deserve my sharing of the roles they played.

A reason for writing about heroism, at least partially, is for those people who have touched my life, and for the children of tomorrow, with the hope that each will live in a world filled with his/her own heroes and heroines providing the light that guides them through the maze of what is becoming a more challenging and complex world.

My students, players on the various teams I've coached, friends in many places, fellow coaches, teachers, and administrators have all been part of my world. I find myself preoccupied by memories of my childhood and friends met along the way, and I have made a special effort to reestablish contact with them, if for no other reason than to let them know how much their presence in my life has meant. All continue to live on in my heart. I hope that they will reflect on the times we shared together, and enjoy some of the tales of earlier times and experiences.

Be watchful of the eyes upon you, young men, and young ladies. There is a good chance that you are a hero or heroine to someone. Don't disappoint.

THE BEGINNING OF A JOURNEY

I've often asked myself why my family began our odyssey from one location to the next over a period of years. There were several possibilities.

Textile mills, like all businesses, were subject to recessions and depressions. Both of my parents worked in various textile plants around the piedmont region of South Carolina, sometimes on different shifts and I'm sure it was difficult to juggle responsibilities at the plant and home. Mother and Dad did have the welfare of four children to consider.

People who worked in the weave room, in any plant, required weavers to achieve a minimum amount of production. If a loom, the machine that weavers were responsible for, broke down, then the loom fixer, who was responsible for repairing the machine, might be repairing another weaver's machine. That meant that someone's machine was left standing and unproductive. It was a common occurrence for a weaver to become irate towards a loom fixer if he felt that his problem was being ignored in favor of another weaver. The weave room boss set a minimum amount of production from every weaver. The plant at Victor was no exception.

When my mother and dad worked at a plant they preferred to work on the same shift and that was not always a preferable arrangement for the plant. There was definitely competition for the jobs as mills began cutting back their workforce.

I sensed that my mother was jealous of other women, at times. When Dad was giving me a ride to school one morning, I made a joke about the three-or four-day growth of his beard. He said that he might not shave again because mother did not like another woman's eyes upon him. We had some interesting discussions at the breakfast table and occasionally that subject surfaced.

The rule "last hired first fired" might have come into effect when plants began to curtail, at times releasing an entire shift, some temporarily.

Whatever the reason(s), we began our trek, as I remember it, in 1945. My mother loved and depended on a lady named Maude Beechum to care for her children while she was working at the Victor plant, located in Greer, S.C. I was sick with pneumonia, according to my eldest sister Jean, and Mother could not entice me to eat for three days, even after a doctor's visit.

Maude, who lived across the nearby Southern Railway tracks, in a black village called Sunnyside, walked into our home on Seventh Street with a boiler of vegetable soup. She said, "Hand me that child." She then sat me on her lap and had me eating her vegetable soup at once. Maude was loved by all, especially me.

I was in the back yard with Maude, one day, as she was bleaching some sheets and white clothing in an old black pot when a young African American girl walked past. I was having a temper tantrum at the time and the girl asked Maude, "Is that child right bright?" According to Jean, who witnessed the event, Maude picked up a rock and chunked it towards the girl, who ran down the street. Our relationship was becoming close.

My dad was given a pump organ and it wound up in Maude's house, since none of us could play it and she, as a very talented musician, would entertain us, as we enjoyed listening to her play the organ and sing. My three sisters and I grew close, as children, to Maude and her family. She really spoiled me on a daily basis, and it was very hard to leave her when we moved, as the Victor plant curtailed a shift and my parents needed to find work.

We left Greer, bound for Iva, S.C., where we lived in a small dwelling for two weeks, until a house became available in Calhoun Falls, where my parents began work. The house in Iva had a tin roof and leaked so badly that we had to put buckets down to catch the rain. A snake had to be removed before we could move in. Calhoun Falls is located next to the Savannah River, which serves as a dividing line between South Carolina and Georgia. I was five years old at the time.

My dad had two uncles, Luke and Earl Bowman, who lived across the river in Georgia and worked in Calhoun Falls.

To supplement their income, they would fish on the Savannah and Broad Rivers. They would then sell their fish, to fish camps, stores, and individuals. Uncle Luke also raised peanuts at the time.

Every year, on July fourth, I would go with my dad to attend a big fish fry, hosted by my relatives from the Georgia side of the Savannah. It was a festive affair and consisted of fried fish, hushpuppies, slaw, potatoes, tea, and beer, with other libations that were brought along. My father, however, did not partake of the alcohol.

The highlight of my trip was watching my uncles grabble for fish, not to be confused with grappling, which requires a large hook. They trapped the fish under a bank or under rocks, as the Savannah River and Broad River both had shoals in certain locations. Underneath the bridge, where U.S Highway 72 crossed the river, consisted of shoals. Not many people grabble for fish these days, but it was common in the '40s and '50s.

There was also a ferry that crossed the Broad River in those days. I remember riding across on the ferry to get to an old country store. RC Colas were five cents. Our trips to the river would continue for years and produced some tall tales and great memories. I always looked forward to July fourth.

After a move back to Victor, where my parents got their jobs back, I started school at Victor Elementary in the summer of 1947, with Mrs. Green as my teacher for two weeks, at which time we moved to Goldville, S.C. We would not return to Victor until 1952.

During a time of constant change, in the southern textile industry, our interesting journey had begun.

Buddy with Grandad and Wilene

JOANNA

As a six-year-old boy, I rarely looked beyond the surface where safety was concerned, choosing to act without considering the consequences. If I asked for permission to take measures then those in power might say no, so why not just act and if the results are not good, then ask forgiveness. Unfortunately, my strategy to behave independently sometimes backfired.

There is no doubt that I was influenced by others in my thinking when I chose to act. I was already an avid cowboy fan. My dad loved western movies and he would take me to a matinee. I would stray to a patch of woods at a very early age and mimic a cowboy by sipping water from a stream. I also sampled wild berries for taste, and without any regard for safety.

It was during a car trip from Anderson, S.C., to Goldville, where my parents worked, that my throat began to tighten and then to feel as though needles were puncturing my throat from the inside. Eventually, each breath took a great amount of effort as my father searched for a doctor. We did find one who gave me a shot which seemed to ease the pain. The doctor diagnosed my condition as diphtheria, and when my father asked how I may have become a victim of the disease he remarked that bad water could have been a contributing factor. I did spend a few days in bed.

The decision to behave independently earned me the name "hardhead", bestowed upon me by my father. He allowed me enough freedom to make many of my own decisions. That was not the case with my mother who reluctantly agreed if I argued well enough and unless it involved money that she was attempting to save. Mother did tan my hide when I used one of her sheets as a cape when I jumped off an outbuilding, playing Superman. There is no doubt that I was wearing on my parents' patience as spankings began to increase. My sisters would sit outside of the room, crying, when I received my punishment. They never had spankings, and it was usually Dad who administered my punishment.

My parents worked at the mill in Joanna, on separate shifts, which was not a favorable situation. "Pug," our Eskimo Spitz breed of dog, amazed us all when he would walk my mother to work in the morning and return to meet her in the afternoon, to accompany her home.

While I lived in Goldville, the name of the town was changed to Joanna. The original name for the town was Martin's Depot. I've already added Joanna to my list of favorite names for towns. Dewy Rose, in Georgia, Bird in Hand and Paradise in Lancaster County, Pennsylvania are others I like.

A favorite memory of Joanna was going to the old Goldville Theater, which still stands today. The theater owner's son, a classmate in the first grade, invited me to the theater for a Saturday of watching movies and eating popcorn. We must have eaten ten boxes of my favorite snack.

Time with my dad watching baseball was another thrilling experience as we watched two local stars, Guy Prater and Joe Prater, play for Joanna. The year in Joanna passed quickly and it was not long thereafter that we left there for Monaghan Mill village, in Greenville, S.C., where my parents would work on the same shift.

Buddy with Wilene and Linda

AROUND THE LOOP

The corner of West Parker Road and Smythe St., at the end of the Monaghan Mill village, located in Greenville, S.C. was where I caught a trolley, which followed a route called *Belt Line North and Belt Line South*. There were other routes around Greenville, S.C., but I knew as a seven-year- old in the schoolyear 1948-49, that I could catch the trolley on the corner, which would then complete the loop and drop me off at the same location from which I started. For me, a new adventure began.

As you stepped onto the trolley, which was shaped like a bus and connected to a cable overhead which provided the electricity, the driver would instruct you to drop a dime into the meter and a token would be provided, which he then dropped into a meter. At that point, the journey began. You could ride all day, if you wished, if you stayed on the trolley.

As the circular tour progressed, we sped past Parker High School and several mill villages, Woodside Mill, Brandon Mill and Judson Mill, located nearby. The Brandon Theater was located near the village after passing under a small railroad bridge, and movies were the main reason for my trips on the trolley.

Brandon is considered the home of the great Shoeless Joe Jackson, who played his first organized baseball there. Jackson and Ty Cobb were my father's favorite baseball players.

My memories today of Brandon Mill Ball Park were from trips as a bat boy for the Victor Pirates. I also played on the field, in my early teens, as an outfielder for the Greer Mill Owls, a team that competed in the Junior Western Carolina League.

When I was told to play right field by Hal Huey, my coach, I had to share the field with a cow that was grazing nearby on grass that needed cutting. She seemed irritated, as I was interfering with her meal. It made my job more difficult, keeping one eye on the cow and the other on the batter. It was also hard to run in the high, uncut grass. And a fresh cow pie also revealed itself at an inopportune time.

Playing on a field with cows was not unusual in those days, as many afternoon games, especially in rural settings, took place in cow pastures, when a regular baseball field was not around. Dried cow chips were used as bases, at times.

It was unusual to have cows inside the city of Greenville, however. It proved difficult to catch fly balls while maneuvering around a bovine which had the best view of the game, next to the umpires and participants.

Today, the realization that I roamed the same turf that Shoeless Joe Jackson once played on at approximately the same age, 14, is special. He began his career there, working in

Brandon Mill, as a sweeper, and the fans passed a hat to collect money during the games in an attempt to keep him.

Leaving the Brandon district, the trolley continued its route through West Greenville, eventually down Pendleton Street and into the town center.

For a while, this section of Greenville fostered a seamy, unattractive side of life, around Pendleton Street. That part of Greenville has since experienced a complete makeover, skyrocketing the aesthetic value of the city.

As one entered the center of Greenville, it was hard to miss the Poinsett Hotel, a beautiful structure on the left, built by John T. Woodside and named for Joel Roberts Poinsett, who was Ambassador to Mexico in 1928 and a world traveler.

The part of the loop that I enjoyed most was the theater district and Greenville had several, located near one another. My favorite theater was the Paris, which featured many *Tarzan* movies, my favorites. Nearby, on the same side of the street was the Center Theater. On the left side of Main Street was the Roxy Theater and the Rivoli Theater, soon to become the Fox Theater. It was nice to have the theaters near one another.

I confess to being smitten by simply entering some of the old movie palaces, with their gorgeous and artistic architecture. It is sad to see old structures, such as theaters and old hotels, destroyed and replaced by other buildings that lack their beauty.

As one entered the theaters, most had carpet, at least in the entrance and corridor. The smell of freshly made popcorn filled the air. In the 1940s, a quarter could buy admission, a box of popcorn and a Coca-Cola for anyone twelve years old and under. An extra nickel could purchase a Butterfinger or Bit-O-Honey.

There was a magnificent old hotel called the Ottaray on Main Street. We ate there once, and the food was delicious. It was about there that the trolley made a left turn, going back toward Monaghan, passing Poinsett, Park Place and Poe Mill.

Greenville had many other businesses downtown, but for me the movie theaters held the most interest. Monaghan held plenty of activities that could interest a young boy, as well. It was a model, in many ways, for many other mill villages around Greenville, due to a man named L.P. "Pete" Hollis. He introduced the YMCA and Boy Scouts of America into the community. He also advanced education among the mill villages.

Parker High School, where my sister Jean went to school at the time, had an excellent sports program, as well. The "Turkey Bowl", a football game which featured Parker High and cross-town rival Greenville High, packed the stands around Thanksgiving.

I had become spoiled, as my mother would say, with all the entertainment and activities close by. As I was to learn quickly, it wouldn't last forever. We would soon find our way to the country, in rural Laurens County, and a sharp contrast in lifestyle.

A YEAR IN TIME OUT

When my family moved to an old house in the country on Teague Road, in Laurens County, S.C., it was a remote spot and offered a sharp contrast to Monaghan Mill village and the business and noisiness of Parker Road in Greenville, S.C.

The sound of cars zooming past in Greenville were replaced by the song of whippoorwills and the whistle of the wind through a grove of hardwoods, near the small house on Teague Road. For a young boy, accustomed to having neighbors nearby, it offered new challenges.

There was electricity running to the small four-room house, in which we lived, but no running water. Our water was drawn from a well and heated in an old black pot, located in the backyard.

For baths, hot water was transferred to a tin tub, which was large enough for an adult if he bent his legs and squeezed into the tub. The girls and I shared water and the Ivory Soap. Wash pans were used for what my mother referred to as "a lick and promise", yesterday's version of the sponge bath.

There was a waterfall amid some woods, not far off, and my dad, Albert Prue Bowman, and I, would occasionally make use of the shower provided by Mother Nature.

Highland Moccasins, also referred to as Copperheads, frequented the area of Laurens Co., and we were always on watch for these venomous snakes on trips to the outhouse, our outside toilet, which was located about 30 yards from the back of the house. Black widow spiders liked outhouses, as well, so every inch of the dwelling was carefully scrutinized before use by our family.

Mother used a wood stove to cook meals. It was there when we moved in and remained so after we left. No one wanted to move a wood stove due to its weight. Some of the best biscuits ever made from plain flour rather than the more popular self-rising flour, were baked in the old stove. It was my job to keep it stocked with wood.

There were few physical hardships on our part. We ate well and slept warm under my mother's handmade quilts after the embers cooled at night in winter. The roots of a pine stump provided the best type of kindling for fires because it contained the most sap, as it trickled down from the top to the roots. This knowledge became helpful as Laurens County had many pine trees. I would chop enough for the family and sell to others who coveted the wood at ten cents for a bundle. Two small pieces of the sap rich kindling were sufficient to start a fire.

A large garden was a luxury for us after having lived around mill villages with limited space. Vegetables and soup mix were put up for the winter and the soil in Laurens County was perfect for cantaloupes and watermelons, which we loved.

My dad came from a family of ten boys and three girls, a total of ten children who lived into adulthood. My mother's family had thirteen children, although two of the siblings died at birth. We had many visiting relatives, as a result. I looked forward to my cousins' visits.

Dad was the eldest of the Bowman children, and we had many who would make the trip from Anderson, S.C., where most of them lived, for Sunday dinner, which was served at noon. Supper was our evening meal. If you stayed for that, it was usually leftovers, assuming there were any. Extended families seemed closer then, and Sundays were for church, visiting relatives and enjoying the time spent with cousins.

My paternal grandfather's Victor Jory-type face, accented with a prominent nose and dark eyes, was typical of the Bowman side of the family. They were passed on to his sons and then to me. He was my main source of male companionship because he shared more time with me than did my father during our stay on Teague Road, as Dad worked extra shifts in the Joanna Textile mill. Boyd Bowman, my grandad, lived with us on Teague Road and added stability, even though he did fight alcohol addiction, as did a couple of my father's uncles. My grandfather and I became very close, even though I would dispose of any booze I found.

My grandfather taught me how to build rabbit gums, which provided our main source of meat. Learning the technique of whistling for bobwhites was fun, as they came closer with each whistle. We didn't shoot them when we drew them close but sharpened our skills in calling them. They once populated our area in great numbers and, sadly, are almost nonexistent in South Carolina today, unless they are raised domestically.

Grandad took me fishing for the first time and scoffed, as I ran into the water in hot pursuit after my first catch, a mud turtle, got off my hook, with me in hot pursuit in an attempt to retrieve it.

A family bonding occurred on Teague Road and some great memories, accompanied by some which were not so great. One of which was the discovery of my shortcomings in math. I was in the third grade at Cross Hill Elementary and struggling with Roman numerals. I don't always remember dreams, but I had one that has lingered in my memory for many years. The scene was a battlefield, and I was alone on one side of it, facing what looked to be a battalion-sized force of Roman numerals. As they marched across the field, the Vs, Xs, IVs, IXs, and others, the bullets just seemed to glance off them, and they continued marching in my direction until, eventually, I fled from them.

To make matters worse, the discipline by my father for my failure to learn Roman numerals caused more stress because he believed that the effort was not there, which might have been true. There is no doubt, however, that the gypsy lifestyle we were leading was already taking its toll on our schoolwork. I also did not possess the math skills of my older sisters, Norma Jean and Sally Wilene.

School became very difficult, despite my sisters' tutoring. Math was a dreaded part of the school day. Spelling, reading, and listening to my grandad read Zane Grey's books became a favorite time of day. He loved visits from the bookmobile that drove by occasionally.

Adjusting to life in a rural setting was tough but some experience was achieved along with some self-reliance and, eventually, a new lifestyle emerged. Bozo, a black, wiry-haired dog who actually belonged to my nearest neighbor was, at least in part, a Water Spaniel. He had boundless energy, and we took to one another instantly, as he was to become a constant companion.

Love for my family was important but I was becoming more independent by the day, as did most boys. There were times when an escape was needed, away from the rule of others, so the idea of building my own hideout, amid some young pine trees, suddenly made sense. They were thick, and concealed, and became a world where only Bozo and I could enter.

Constructing a lean-to, made from pine limbs and with pine needles to rest on, added warmth and comfort. It was an escape from parents, older sisters and with rules of my own. Bozo became my best friend and my first soulmate. Maybe all young people need their own hideouts to feed their self-concept and begin creating their own world. There were times when I would sneak off from the old house on a moonlit night and sleep on the pine needles, with Bozo beside me.

Today, I find young people depending on others to cure their boredom. Living in Monaghan, I could always wander up the street to play cowboys with a classmate, dressing up in the Roy Rogers outfit that was a Christmas gift, or I could walk down to the YMCA.

The radio did provide a source of entertainment. After supper, the family would gather to listen to the radio. Inner Sanctum was a popular program that would keep us on the edge of our seats.

My personal favorites were "The Lone Ranger" and boxing, listening as my hero, Joe Louis, was defeated by Ezzard Charles in 1950. I ran from the house, in tears, because Joe Louis was the champ, an institution, and invincible. I wouldn't pull for another heavyweight boxer until Rocky Marciano took the crown.

Radio didn't provide images, thereby allowing one's imagination to flourish, wondering about the physical appearances of Jack Benny, his sidekick, Rochester, and of Amos and Andy and their friend Kingfish, a hilarious character, on the comedies we all enjoyed.

At least the image of The Lone Ranger could be found in comic books. Radio, otherwise, allowed you to create your own. Bill Reeder, my sister Jean's future husband, was a rescuer from boredom when he visited. He was following in the footsteps of his father, who was a skilled carpenter. Bill would eventually own a construction business, and build his own home, before turning twenty-one.

At the time, he owned a 1929 Ford convertible that, even then, was an antique. It was a beautifully painted brown and tan two-seater, with a rumble seat in the rear, in which I thoroughly enjoyed riding. Bill was the ultimate, fast driving car enthusiast, and it wasn't very long before he traded the A Model for a 1939 Ford.

His car always had a good radio and was tuned into country music stations with songs like, "Hey Good Looking" and other hits by Hank Williams, who was most people's favorite at the time. Country music and Blue Grass ruled the day, although swing was still around.

People from lower economic classes seemed to identify with country music. Permeated with loneliness, while sitting on a bench, built by my grandfather and located in the midst of the grove of hardwood trees, perhaps gave me too much time to reflect.

I would sing a song recorded by Hank Williams entitled "I'm So Lonesome I Could Cry," and at times I did cry. He was my favorite singer, at the time. When I hear the words to that song today, it reminds me of Teague Road.

Yep, Hank Williams had that ability to tap into my soul. Thankfully, it was also his music that raised my spirit. Before Elvis, there was Hank, as a singer and song writer.

Stock car racing was just arriving on the scene and, along with it, a fire and passion among the masses in the rural southeast, in particular, the bootleggers. Going home with friends from church for Sunday dinner, stock car racing and drive-in movies with Bill, provided a break from my seclusion on Teague Road. He became a big brother.

My favorite pastime was swimming, and begging someone to take me to a river became a habit, since there were no pools around. Bill took me to a rock quarry, a small lake that was fed by a nearby spring, and located in Laurens County, near Cold Point. It was clear and cold, and the elevated rocks offered a perfect platform for diving. It was there that I became the Johnny Weissmuller version of Tarzan, diving off a cliff somewhere in Africa, even though the movies were actually filmed, partially, somewhere in Florida.

My family, the Reeder family, my relatives, and especially a dog named Bozo were a big part of the "time out" portion of my life, located on Teague Road. The worst part of leaving there was to learn that my best friend would not be coming along. I suspected that my neighbors would not allow him to leave, even though he spent the majority of his time by my side.

Bozo and Me

Across the field he rambled, visible, then disappearing,
His head bobbing up, then down, as if swimming a breaststroke.
Through a sea of oats and into my life, he came.

He conquered me with a love like no other, my best friend,
My only friend, in a solitary land,
The rabbits, the foxes, the oat fields, the whip o' wills,
The bobwhites, Bozo and me.

Through the days we played, in the woods, by the stream,
Across the field, by the pond. In the nights we talked, as he
Lay by my open window, though he mostly listened.

At times we slept in our hideout, secluded, among the young pines,
Lying on a soft bed of pine needles. He was my constant companion,
My protector, the keeper of our secrets and I knew that one day it
Would end.

    As quickly as he came into my life, we parted,
And through teary eyes from the back window of a 41 Chevy,
I saw his black head bobbing in the oat field, as I left my best friend
Behind.

MAIN STREET, CROSS HILL

Cross Hill was where my family moved from Monaghan Mill Village, in 1949. It is a very small town in Laurens County, about 50 miles south of Greenville, S.C. State Highway 39 breaks off Highway 221 and then crosses U.S. Highway 72, where it becomes Main Street, Cross Hill, with the street widening as you travel through town.

Old houses, a few with gables and extended porches, and remnants of other grand homes, in decay or demolished, add the appearance of an untold past of Main Street, where most of the more prominent members of the community resided and where a few, defined by ethnicity, occupation, and of course, the necessary income, could rent or purchase.

In 1903, Cross Hill boasted of five doctors, a school, and around twenty businesses, which included a bank, a drugstore, a cotton gin, an oil mill, a hotel, boarding houses, general merchandise stores and a post office. A major railroad ran through Cross Hill and transported passengers to a drop-off for the Harris Springs Hotel, outside of town, renowned as a resort destination for the northern elite.

Throughout the country, at that time, there were "watering places," where people went to recover their health, since it was considered sinful, by many, to take vacations, living by the adage, "idleness is the devil's workshop."

The minerals in the water at Harris Springs were considered unique, containing healing properties. There were several springs located around the Piedmont region of South Carolina that claimed to have special qualities that might nurse one back to health. Cross Hill, in 1903, was a thriving little community but evidence of that is not there today.

Coleman's grocery was the first business that I noticed, and it was located on the corner of U.S. Highway 72 and state Highway 39. I remembered it best for the ice cream cones, which were great. Leaman Brothers Hardware, Dry Goods and Grocery Store was where we picked up our mail. It was a large store at that time and a center of economic activity for the town. Ed Leaman, a young boy who was almost a year older than I, and the son of Sam and Helen Griffin Leaman, became my best friend.

Our family first lived, temporarily, in one half of an old store building, since we needed more space. Then, since we moved to Teague Road, a few miles out of town, before moving back to Cross Hill, we eventually moved into the old Guthrie house, which had an upstairs and above that, an attic. It was also located on Main Street, an older house, even for that time. The house had a rustic charm and I enjoyed living there. You'll see an overgrown lot if you drive by it today. The first night in the old house was an adventure. The house was large enough for me to have my own room.

Soon after we moved in, Linda, the youngest of my sisters, and Wilene, who was next to me in age, came running down the stairs to my room screaming during the night that the house was haunted. We went up to their rooms, and there was, indeed, the sound of footsteps overhead. Both refused to sleep upstairs.

The drama continued until the next morning, when we went outside and looked up towards the attic and discovered a hole in the woodwork and, as if on cue, several buzzards began flying out, so we had discovered our ghosts. Lake Greenwood, located nearby, was referred to as "Buzzard's Roost" and had a fairly large population of the birds. Late in the evening, it seemed like they were blackening the sky as they flew to their roosts.

Cross Hill had an elementary school, which had once served as a high school. It was in the Clinton High School district. My sister Jean finished Clinton High School. Eleanora Major, who became the second wife of Jimmy Hollingsworth was the Principal of Cross Hill Elementary and, my teacher in both the third and fourth grades.

Realizing that an eight or nine-year-old boy's assessment of a teacher is not very reliable, especially after the passing of 65+ years, I still say there were a couple of things concerning the lady that stood out.

In an age when teachers and principals made use of the strap, as a means of discouraging bad behavior, she was definitely a proponent of and very efficient at performing such a method. I probably came out ahead by committing more mischievous deeds than those for which I received such punishment.

Miss Major was also a lady who would display great kindness. The school had a variety show in which she auditioned me for a part. I was to appear on stage, for the first time, performing a monologue of a young boy, with his face blackened, describing Noah as he loaded animals onto the ark. She worked on the part with me for days and the show was a huge success, as the community packed the small auditorium. Miss Major praised me for my effort.

Since Cross Hill Baptist Church had burned, the school auditorium was used for church services. Liberty Hill Presbyterian Church, located in Cross Hill, was also very cooperative with and sympathetic to the Baptists when the fire occurred. Scottish Presbyterians were among the founders of Cross Hill, that dated back to before the American Civil War, but there is still some uncertainty concerning the original founders.

Life in the small town would have been dismal without my friend, Ed Leaman, and the Wilkie boys, Marshall, also known as Chuck, and Ralph, who would someday marry my youngest sister, Linda.

Ralph and Chuck were both older than I and their family supplemented their income by selling fishing bait to anglers who were headed to the lake. Without an abundance of events taking place in the small town, I enjoyed wading up streams with the boys and seining for minnows. We also caught spring lizards, which were in great demand.

The Wilkies had beautiful children, and Ralph, with his good build and bronze complexion, had a nice smile, John F.

Kennedy type hair and deep, penetrating blue eyes. Those eyes would eventually become too much for my sister to resist.

Ed Leaman and I spent every available moment together. Helen Griffin Leaman, Ed's mother, was a delightful lady who allowed me to visit on occasion, but both Ed and I enjoyed time in the wild. We had our own hideout in a nearby wooded area. I never felt the contrast of wealth between our families from Ed but straying outside of my comfort zone into unfamiliar territory, with a feeling of uncertainty existing, did create some uneasiness on my part, although Ed seemed at home in any situation.

There were those who reached out to our family and included us in their lives. There were also a few who were reluctant to accept outsiders. The Rasor family was one of the earliest families in Cross Hill, and in an age when there was a custom of inviting friends for a Sunday meal after church, I was afforded the opportunity to know Jake Rasor, Jr. The family owned a home at Harris Springs and had a very comfortable lifestyle.

I did not concern myself with their financial success at the time, and Jake Rasor became a good friend, and we enjoyed running around the home, built with rock, playing cowboys, and shooting cap pistols at one another. He would later finish college, become a high school band director, and then run the family business.

It was in the Rasor household that I ate my first Baked Alaska, an angel food cake with frozen strawberries and ice cream in the center. As I began to use my fork to cut into the dessert, the cake slipped off my plate, went flying through the air and landed in front of Mr. Rasor. He smiled and said, "I believe it can be retrieved," and then placed it back on my plate, which I was hiding behind, with embarrassment.

Caroline Motes Rasor, Jake's mother, was a woman of many talents when dealing with children and her genuine compassion was exhibited through her kind deeds. She was full of energy and very pleasant, always willing to share her time.

I'm not sure how we were able to teach ourselves to harmonize but Linda, Wilene and I could pick out the soprano, alto and tenor parts with ease, even though none of us could read music. Caroline spent endless hours with us in the newly built Cross Hill Baptist Church, as she was both an accompanist and teacher of music. She was responsible for developing our talents.

In our first appearance before an audience, the three of us experienced stage fright and our once bold voices, that rang out in practice, became very timid, with Caroline whispering, "Sing out, sing out." So much for debuts, as three big-eyed kids were relieved to exit the stage.

Life lacked the luster and excitement of some communities around Cross Hill, but it had a quality that many other places I lived in did not possess and that was a chance to commune with nature on a daily basis. There were streams, the lake, fields, and woods around, in abundance. Relationships became even more important and fostered creativity.

There were plenty of activities that did not cost money, such as becoming mesmerized by, and catching, fireflies, watching trains pass, counting the numbers, sitting on the front porch of Pappy Burns, an elderly gentleman who lived nearby, and listening to his stories, and even making friends with a hog, since my dad kept warning me that once cold weather rolled around there were other plans for him.

I collected, and traded, discarded comic books, and found very interesting the ones depicting the Korean War. The American soldiers appeared to be clean cut, while the Red Chinese and North Koreans had evil eyes and smiles. The war propaganda was used to influence American opinion.

I could earn a little money during the fall, picking cotton, with no cotton-picking machines around. Time spent alone while poking the cotton in my burlap bag gave me an abundance of time to think, which sometimes got me in trouble. The going rate for picking cotton was two cents per pound, paid by the cheapskates, and three cents per pound by the more humane. A fellow could earn four cents per pound if the cotton was picked once, and you would pick it again for the tidbits. I picked cotton to earn money to go to the Anderson County Fair, the best fair in the state of South Carolina, because it represented about five counties at the time. I could walk to the fair from my Grandmother Bowman's home on Rosewood Avenue, in Anderson, S.C.

During the summer, I picked blackberries and sold them in small amounts. There were several ladies in town, like Mrs. Ruth Sharpe, who would pay me ten cents to pick enough for a cobbler. I had people looking me up, so I'm sure I was charging too little, but a dime bought a couple of candy bars in those days, or a hotdog from Cromer's, which I loved.

Snakes and briars kept most people away from picking blackberries. Black snakes, green snakes and king snakes were the most frequent visitors in a blackberry patch. I've had them crawl near me through the brambles and I was glad to have company because they kept poisonous snakes away.

Boredom in an active, young boy's life can cause problems. My sister Jean had a nice pair of roller skates that I borrowed occasionally. One summer night, as her boyfriend, Bill Reeder, was leaving, I had a notion, not properly conceived, to grab hold of the back bumper of his 1939 Ford and hitch a ride while wearing Jean's skates. They were not built to keep up with Bill's V-8.

As young lads feel compelled to show off in front of their girlfriends, at times, Bill slid into his role as Lee Petty and proceeded in a reckless manner up Main Street, with haste, not knowing that I was trailing behind, attached to his bumper on Jean's roller skates.

Luckily, with it being a warm summer night, Bill had his windows down and heard my screams, as I was afraid to turn loose of the bumper. By the time he stopped, the skates were smoking. I expected a severe scolding from Bill as he walked to the rear, but his wide-eyed appearance communicated a look of disbelief, as he shook his head and was speechless. It was probably the most exciting moment of my life, up to that point.

I would imagine that some other 9-year-old boys had a fascination for a girl that he kept secret. Mine was an autumn haired girl named Rett McGowan, who was a year older than me and whose mother taught the fifth grade at Cross Hill Elementary School. The reason my secret remained so is that I had freckles and I considered myself ugly. Others kidded me about the freckles with remarks like, "You swallowed a dollar, and it broke out in pennies." I was also very shy around girls at the time.

Like my father, I wore overalls and one of my galluses was broken on them. During the summer, the denim legs were rolled up to run faster and no shoes or shirts were worn, of course, except to school. Miracles do occur, however, and I offered to carry her books home from school one day and a friendship developed. I lived, for a while, across the street from her.

One summer morning, Mrs. McGowan knocked on our door and invited me to their home to watch a movie on their 8 mm projector. The invitation was accepted, of course, because I really missed going to movie theaters and summertime boredom was setting in.

Mrs. McGowan offered some vegetable soup for lunch, and I accepted. I had only experienced my mother's homemade soup and it was unique to try something different. It was made by Heinz. After lunch, she told us we could go outside and play, and I was in a quandary as to the type of activities boys and girls could do together. Linda had gotten a tea set for Christmas, and I would sit around with her at one of her tea parties, at times, pretending to eat cookies and sip tea. Rett taught me how to play hopscotch so that solved the problem. I loved the old home in which they lived.

Ed Leaman told me later that a murder had taken place in the old house in which the McGowans lived, and you could hear spooky sounds around the property during full moons. He said that there was a board in the house that you could raise that was bloodstained underneath. Ed was the best at adding drama. He told many suspenseful stories that kept me entertained.

After I left Cross Hill in 1951, I wondered what happened to Rett, who lost both of her parents not long afterward and went to live with relatives. The name, McGowan, goes back to the founding of Cross Hill. McGowans even fought in the American Revolution.

Living by a railroad, it was not unusual for hoboes, people who sneaked on trains for a ride, to visit our home. My mother fed more than one, usually having him sit on the back steps to eat his meal, after performing a chore, such as chopping wood. Mother had a strong recollection of the Great Depression, since it was in the recent past and more people hoboed trains as a means of travel. She also hated to see anyone go hungry.

Cross Hill, during its post-World War II years, was inhabited by some tough, hardworking people. They had just experienced adversity, both abroad and at home. When conflict arose, there were times when it was settled with fists. Youngsters would settle conflict in a similar manner, before or after school, knowing that they would have to bend over the principal's desk to receive their punishment, for fighting. You learned how to defend yourself or suffer abuse at the hands of others. I held my own but preferred to avoid harm's way.

Some workers might end a tough week by getting rid of some frustrations with a cold glass of beer in a tavern around Cane Creek, located on Lake Greenwood. People worked and played hard, and sometimes, a night would end up with a fight and someone getting shot or cut. Others would be in church praying for those who visited such establishments.

My sister Linda, who years later married Ralph Wilkie after her sophomore year at Greer High and gave birth to their two children, Steve and Lyn, became a widow at a very early age. Ralph and Bill Reeder were out for a drink in a bar in Greenwood when Ralph was involved in an altercation with a man. The bartender, attempting to break up the fight, shot and killed Ralph. The bartender was sentenced to eighteen years in prison for voluntary manslaughter.

There were many good people in Cross Hill, but my associations were limited to a few. The Reeders, Bill's family, were wonderful. Jean, Joyce, Nannie Belle, Mills, who was a close friend, and Josephine, the youngest, all treated us like family.

Mr. Reeder, Bill's dad, would buy a popular boat landing at Cauthrens Bridge, on Lake Greenwood. As a teenager, I watched as the famous baseball player, Ted Williams, put his boat in the water at Reeder's Landing and he was nice enough to give me his autograph.

Mother gave birth to my baby brother, James Boyd, and Jean married Bill Reeder before we left Cross Hill. It felt strange leaving her behind. There were times when she assumed my mother's role when she was working. Their first home was in Ninety- Six, S.C.

Cross Hill, like Teague Road, provided a change in lifestyle but it was special, and I have wonderful memories of both. I enjoyed the experiences and most of the relationships that I encountered. Life was simple and at times I felt isolated, but I also left there more independent.

Throughout my life, I've found myself taking detours just to travel through Cross Hill to visit my friend Lois Austin. She was a local historian and could always keep me up to date on happenings around Cross Hill. I also stop by to visit Chuck Wilkie, whom I consider to be a family member.

Occasionally I also take in a service at Cross Hill Baptist Church, which will always hold special memories. Cross Hill is, and always will be, a part of me. As we moved our last possessions out of the town in 1951, I remember the sad expression of Ed Leaman, as we waved to one another for the last time. I would miss my old friend.

Buddy with Linda, Wilene, and cousin Mary Sue

THE DOWNS AND UPS OF A MID-CENTURY

In that summer of 1951, I felt like a world traveler with a migrant worker lifestyle. With the growing unemployment of mill workers and for other reasons, my family was beginning a new adventure with a move to a community above Greer, S.C. but leaving good friends behind was heart-wrenching. My sisters and I were to attend three different schools in the school year 1951-52, a turbulent, sometimes devastating, but also rewarding time.

Jordan

The Jordan community located a few miles from Greer up Highway 14, and the next stop on our journey, presented yet another challenge for me. I had finished, without complete success, my fourth year of school at Cross Hill and then began the fifth grade, with a new school and people.

We had a short stay in the community and school was the main focus of my activities. Recess, as usual, was my favorite part of the school day. The trees at the edge of the playground at

Jordan Elementary provided some of the best mountain apples anywhere, and baseball, America's main sport in the day, was always present, if a bat and ball could be found.

The Jordan farming co-op, an institution typical of many rural areas, was located across the street from the school. It provided locker space for meat storage and provided other services, as well. There were many co-ops that dotted the maps of rural America and usually they were the least expensive way for a farmer or others to store or buy goods. The main purpose of the co-op was to save member patrons money, not to make money.

A Hero Emerges

We had not settled in good until my parents informed my sisters and me that our four-month-old brother, James, was seriously ill with a liver disease. My parents spent endless hours at the hospital, and Dad continued to work until he and Mother entered the home one day, sat us down, and broke the news that we had lost James.

James Boyd Bowman, in the five months that he lived, had won the hearts of each family member. It was a tragic blow. I loved all my sisters, but I had looked forward to having a brother around, and the news sent our family into a downward spiral.

It was an old Southern Baptist tradition to take food to the families who lost loved ones and the people of Jordan were very giving, in so many ways.

Lewis Phillips, a man with the most honest face and sincerest eyes that, to this day, I remember, showed up on our doorstep and informed us that we would not have to worry about paying for books, a kind gesture on his behalf. Little did I know, at the time, the important role he was to play in my life.

Coach Phillips, who would have his start teaching and coaching at Jordan High School, would later become my basketball and football coach at Greer High. He was a World War II veteran who fought in North Africa, Italy and France and had been wounded in combat. He was in a military hospital when he opened his eyes and thought, for sure, that he had died and gone to heaven, because standing over him was the most beautiful angel he could have wished for. His nurse, Elma Bailey, would later become his wife.

The timing for a hero in my life was perfect then, and he was to reappear, time and again, throughout my young life, just as he helped the lives of so many others. My school year at Jordan was disrupted, after James' death, as my sisters and I were sent to Anderson to live with our grandmother for a few weeks. We attended East Whitner Elementary School there.

The Christmas of 1951 did not begin with smiling faces. There were many medical expenses, and my dad and mom were proud people who would never default on a debt. For that reason, the cupboard was pretty bare that Christmas.

Suddenly the door opened and there stood my sister Jean, and her husband, Bill Reeder, with bags full of toys and goodies. A feeling of togetherness filled the room that Christmas, as we read scriptures and sang carols. We enjoyed the love for one another, and it was a great way to end the year.

Victor Opens its Arms

We moved back to Victor in January of 1952 into a small house on Forrester St., below Victor Mill Village, until my parents bought the house on 22nd Street. I started school at Victor Elementary in the middle of the fifth grade. At this point, with events transpiring the way they had during the year 1951, I felt sad and beaten down, but, after the move, a sense of permanence began to emerge. The trek, it seemed, had ended. A heroine also came into my life.

Margaret Bull, my new teacher, was an on-task, organized lady whose interesting class was heightened even more by her talent of solving what was extremely difficult to a fifth-grader, using simplistic methodology and by translating her lessons into a language that even the slowest math student in class, that being me, I'd guess, could understand.

I can still recall her standing tall as she explained the function of a numerator as we were studying fractions. She would then bend her knees and make herself shorter as she explained the role of a denominator. Previously, I had confused the two, but never again.

My favorite part of the new school was the last part of the day, when she read to us from a Hardy Boys mystery. She would always stop at a very interesting part, saying, "and we will pick up there tomorrow." She turned me on to reading and I began trips to the school library.

At the end of the school year came our end of the year party, which was held at Chick Springs, owned, and operated by my teacher, Miss Bull, and her family. It was a swimming lake, fed by a natural spring, without chlorination, as some pools had, and was located on U.S. Highway 29, also referred to as the Super Highway in 1952, close to the small town of Taylors.

While swimming, a classmate ran out of the water yelling "Snake! Snake!" Miss Bull just waded into the pool, plucked the reptile from the water, smiled as the snake wiggled in her hand and proclaimed that it was just a harmless water snake. She instructed us, "There are at least 50 nonpoisonous varieties around." The lady stood 9 feet tall in my eyes. What a way to end a school year.

I'm sure we all have a favorite teacher, but the timing could not have been better for the presence of such a fine teacher into my life. I looked forward to school because of her and, although I was far behind in some studies, I felt like I was resolving some math issues.

Music also reentered my life as the principal of Victor Elementary, Edward Schingler, formed the Victor Boys Choir, later to become the Kiwanis Boys Choir. I auditioned and was accepted into the choir. Music would always place a smile on my face, and we sang both secular and religious songs when we appeared before the public. Some friendships were born in that year that have lasted a lifetime.

1951-52 had dark moments but it was also a time of acceptance, accompanied by the feeling that we, as a family, had returned home. Victor had opened its arms.

ED LEAMAN

I was almost eleven years old, and my family was living on Forrester Street, located off McDaniel Avenue, in Greer, when my oldest sister, Jean, paid us a visit in March 1952. She did not smile, upon entering the small house, and looked directly at me, with a grimace, as if she regretted the purpose of her visit.

We sat at the kitchen table and Jean, typically straight to the point, broke the news that Ed Leaman, my dear friend from Cross Hill, who was 11 years old, had passed away.

She was told that he had taken his own life, with his father's pistol, revealing that a reason could have been because of grades, quoting secondary sources, as she had received the news from neighbors of the family.

Stunned by the news, I ran to James woods, located at the edge of Victor mill village, my place of solitude and reflection, and grieved in private. My parents were always understanding regarding my response to a loss and allowed me my space and time to recover.

I remember Ed as a brilliant boy, extremely gifted and full of energy. I still have a hard time accepting his death, due to the nature of his demise and his young age leaving this world. He was very creative and planned many of our activities, which cost no money, because my family spent nothing on toys. We found an old baby buggy and made a wagon with wheels, a rope, some scrap wood, nails, and other necessary items that we were able to find. We made sling shots from a prong, cut from a sapling, rubber from an old inner tube and the tongue from an old shoe.

Most memorable of all were his stories, told as if he were on stage, and I was always a willing audience. We picked and smoked rabbit tobacco in an old corncob pipe and waded in streams that fed into Lake Greenwood. I think just being around one another and enjoying the other's company was enough to form strong memories.

· After Margaret Bull, my fifth-grade teacher at Victor Elementary, turned me on to reading, she recommended that I read the *Adventures of Tom Sawyer*. I believe I eventually chose to read the rest of Mark Twain's books because the characters reminded me of the relationship that Ed and I had experienced, with Ed as Tom and I, with my torn overalls, supported by one strap, no shoes and summertime dirty feet, as Huck Finn.

My experiences with Ed would follow me forever and cause many tears, even today. There are times when I picture him, as I did in a dream once, on a raft, looking back at me, ready to explore the next bend in the river.

I'm still haunted by my memory of Ed, and his life-ending episode would influence me, as a teacher years later. I would stand by my doorway, greet, and then gaze into the eyes of every student who passed to enter, searching for a look in any of them that would give away any hint of stress in their lives, any unhappiness.

A student who was zoned out, head down, lacking interaction and, of course, the absence of a smile, gave clues as one who could be experiencing problems. Today, as I watch loved ones and friends succumb to poor health, after living a rich, full life, I've learned to accept that, one by one, the time will come for each of us, but when someone leaves us at an early age, due to an accident and especially by choice, as Ed did, it is unsettling and hard to bear.

We relive the trauma, wondering how we might have steered the victim in another direction, away from that fatal decision. I've never left Cross Hill, in spirit, completely. I still carry it with me, the pleasant memories and the sad memories, as well, which I know will remain with me forever.

I'LL ALWAYS BE A VICTOR BOY

Today the presence of spirits is felt, as I come upon the triangle formed by what is known as Victor Avenue and Old Woodruff Road, in Greer, S.C. The old entrance to Victor Mill Village has taken on a different appearance and, with it, an emptiness. An emptiness of youth, of voices and images, long past.

The two evergreens that once adorned the walkway to the YMCA, one on each side, are not there. The shuffleboard, once close to them and was used by the older citizens of Victor, no longer exists. Neither does the YMCA, the Community building, which stood beside it, the company store, and the Esso station up Victor Avenue. The mill itself, once owned by J.P. Stevens, has not even the remnants left. The water tower has vanished. The memories remain, pleasant ones, for the most part, and a bonding of friendships, several that last to this day and seem to increase in importance, as our numbers are dwindling.

As you entered the YMCA, in 1952, there was a Coca-Cola machine on the immediate right that issued a soft drink, often referred to by boys as a dope, or belly washer, with the flip of a handle, if one was fortunate enough to possess the required six cents. You could also journey up to the company store or Esso station, for a Pepsi or RC Cola, both of which had 12 ounces, instead of the smaller six-ounce Coke. You might share the contents with a buddy if the friend called "dibs" first.

The trophy case, also near the entrance of Victor YMCA, revealed the athletic success of past years, identifying Victor as a community of champions. It served as a reminder to visiting teams that walking out of the building with a win would prove difficult. Victor was very competitive. The trophies presented a vision and a challenge to the younger boys and girls coming up.

There was the checker room, if you turned right at the trophy case, which was usually occupied by senior citizens who lived in Victor. Beside the checker room was a Ping-Pong room, where the girls loved to visit and participate.

The sports competitiveness was strong around Greer, S.C., with mill villages like Apalache, Greer Mill, Franklin, Pelham, Lyman, Taylors, and Victor beginning play at an early age. No young boys or girls were turned away, regardless of where they lived. All were invited to participate. By the time the athletes who lived in these mill villages entered Greer High, they were ready to compete in Greer High sports. In short, the mills provided many fine athletes for the area high schools, not only around Greer but in places like Greenville and towns all over the southeastern United States.

Other mill villages in the piedmont region of S.C. had many of the same structures and lifestyles, with each having its own memories. Monaghan, Dunean, Woodside, Brandon, Poe, and Judson in Greenville, were good examples. Towns like Spartanburg, Easley, Piedmont, Pelzer, Anderson, Clinton, Joanna and Greenwood all had sports teams.

Victor YMCA sponsored a team for young girls and had some good teams. Basketball was the only team sport in which they participated, at this time. That did not stop them from hanging out at the "Y", observing games and practices in which the boys were participating. Some were, perhaps, just boy-watching.

The focus of young girls, for the most part, seemed different but perhaps that was because they were not allowed as many options since it was the YMCA. Some loved playing with dolls and reading but would occasionally join the boys around Victor in a pickup game of baseball. The girls' basketball teams at Victor competed well, winning the Jr. Southern Textile Basketball Tournament in Greenville, one year, amidst stiff competition.

There was a time when the gym floor was used for roller skating. Every Halloween featured kids dressing up and skating. Boxing and wrestling matches were also held there. Linda Bruce remembers when her mother, a seamstress, made costumes for her to wear while skating. One year, she went to a Halloween event as a yellow butterfly.

Upon entering the door of the gym, there was the smell of a freshly polished, wooden floor, as great care was taken in the upkeep of the entire structure, the pride of the community. No street shoes were allowed on the floor. It was sneakers or socks.

On Saturdays I participated in ping-pong doubles with Pat Cox, who was my partner, against friends Judy Owens and Mack Allen. The girls would show up in rolled up jeans and bobby sox, ready to compete. Both eventually married Victor boys. Pat married Jack McKinney and Judy married Bobby Gravley. Judy also became an avid tennis player, so perhaps table tennis at the Y created her interest in the sport.

In the basement of the Y were the bathrooms and showers. My first trip ever to a YMCA was with my father, to take a shower. This was a luxury, as few, if any, homes were equipped with a shower. Upon request, we were tossed a towel to promote personal hygiene. After each team practice, we were told to hit the shower.

The squeaking of sneakers, better known as tennis shoes in the day, could be heard and the voices of kids having fun, haunting sounds, ingrained forever. Those sounds were contagious and set the mood for the day. The Y was a happy place.

No one could ask for a better coach than Leon Gravley, mainly because of his patience. He was the Victor Assistant Athletic Director at the time. As an 11-year-old, I played my first game of organized basketball at Victor, with Leon as my coach. I thought that I knew the basic rules but there was still much for me to learn about the game.

During a timeout, Leon motioned for me to enter a game, which was my first time, ever. He explained that I would be playing guard. When the other team had the ball, I guarded my man closely. I would have followed him to the water fountain and back. When we had the ball, I was still guarding my man closely. The boy I was guarding asked, "What are you doing? Your team has the ball!" A patient Leon called timeout and explained to me that when we had the ball I could dribble and shoot. "Then why do they call me a guard?" I asked. He laughed and set me at ease, assuring me that it was fine to mess up occasionally. I was happy that I was allowed to shoot.

Fred Snoddy was the Athletic Director at Victor. A University of South Carolina graduate, where he played end for the Gamecocks, he was also my first football coach and designated me as an end. He set a fine example for those who visited the YMCA, as did many of the older boys. No membership was required in those days. We just showed up. It was J.P. Stevens & Co. who picked up the tab.

One summer afternoon I was hanging around the gym, mainly to practice my ball handling without anyone around, as I did make mistakes and didn't want people to see them. Not many kids liked to be inside a gym, sweating, during hot weather, but I found it rewarding to have the gym to myself. Fred asked me to run an errand for him and I obliged.

He gave me an envelope, then asked me to walk to the bank, uptown, and deposit it for him. Then, presenting a dime, he told me to walk back by Ponders and buy an ice cream for myself. The ice cream was a nice gesture, but I've relived that moment many times and the fact that he put his trust in me warmed my heart, as it still does today. It feels nice to be trusted.

Those two men, and the athletic directors who followed, set fine examples for all of us, as did the older guys around Victor, like Butch Miller, who would someday become the athletic director at both Victor and Greer Mill. The Y was not just a building we frequented, it was a brotherhood and sisterhood. We looked out for one another. When any age group played, we were in the stands for one another's games.

The Stewart boys, Joe, Duck and Gundy, were very special to me, and I attended their games even after they moved on to Greer High, where all excelled. One time Duck was playing against Dunean in a Biddy Boys basketball game and Victor was winning by one point, and after a jump ball, he dribbled down and scored a basket for the other team, just before the final buzzer. He was crushed, after his mistake. Along with others, I assured him that Victor would not have been in the game if not for his efforts. We cheered each other on but we were always there to pick one another up when we gave our best effort and came up short.

While we did support one another, we also expected the best effort from each other. Lessons were also learned. Good behavior was expected, as well. One day, as I was gamboling up the steps to the Y and speaking a bit profanely, Lewis Garrett, an older boy, grabbed my arm and pointed it toward the letters, YMCA, above the entrance. Lewis asked if I understood the significance of those letters. I replied that I didn't, and I promptly received a lesson in values and prosperity that I still remember and expound.

The most important function of the Y, from my viewpoint, years down the road and after the fact, is that our parents knew where they would find us, and it must have given them a sense of security knowing that their children were being supervised by upstanding people.

While the use of the term *progress* is associated with making the world a better place in which to live, I'm sure that the young people who walked up those steps to the Y would agree that our children and grandchildren have nothing close to what we experienced, a refuge for the ones who needed it most. It has proven to be lifechanging for some.

Boys are never completely behaved, and pranks were common during the 1950s. There were initiations, which today would be considered as hazing. We shrugged it off, not feeling personally violated or traumatized. If one played on a basketball team, for instance, before each practice he was issued a pair of socks, a jock (athletic supporter) and basketball shorts. When I asked about the use of a jock, not ever having seen or used one, one of the older guys was happy to instruct me on its use, placing it over my head and protecting my nose. I eventually figured out its purpose and the guys had a good laugh.

The rafters in the gym were strong enough to support the roof and a young boy's pants, which were tossed up there, occasionally. They didn't voluntarily come down and if you wanted them, you climbed up on the rafters to retrieve them. It was not unusual to exit the showers and find your clothes missing. If one became upset, then he was a candidate for another prank. The best response was to calmly wrap your towel around your midsection and start searching for your clothes, sometimes finding them outside the Y, perhaps on a bush.

The young girls who lived around Victor were also candidates for pranks. Girls wore sashes on their dresses, which were tied in a bow behind the dress. Laveda Bruce was the victim of a prank when she was tied by the sashes of her dress to a Chinaberry tree that stood in front of Bruce's Lunch, and she screamed for someone to set her free. Billy Gravley was the perpetrator of the prank, but all had a good laugh.

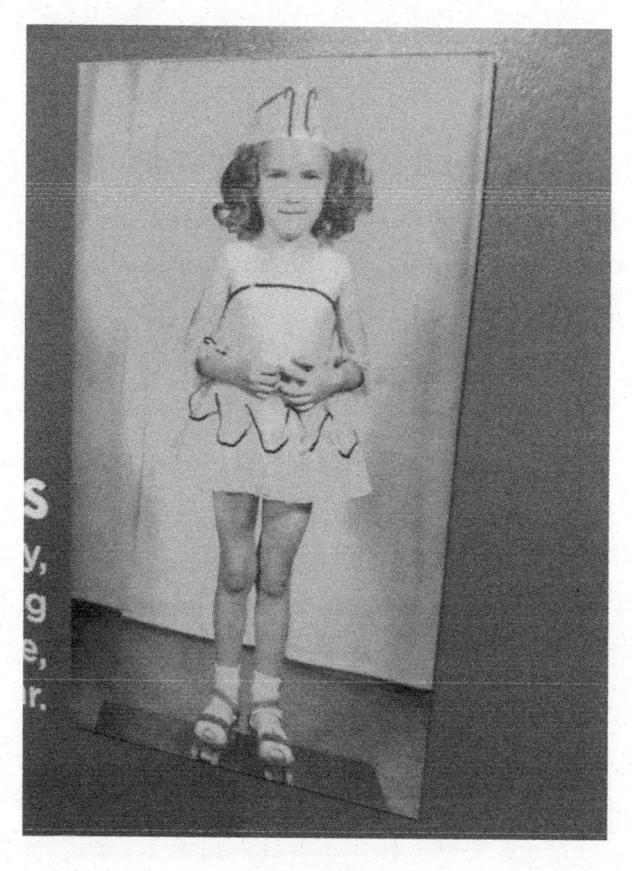

Linda Bruce

1950 Victor Midget Basketball Team

First Row (left to right): Jack McKinney, Bobby Gravley, Dicky Gravley, Gary Vaughn, Joel Hendrix

Second Row (left to right): Coach Leon Gravley, Butch Miller, Darrel Leonhardt, Steve Satterfield, Mickey Bomar, Jimmy Owensby

Our Own Version of March Madness

Each mill village had its teams, and they were showcased when the Southern Textile Basketball Tournament was held in Greenville, S.C. Teams from Alabama, Tennessee, Florida, North Carolina, and Georgia came to compete on several different age levels. eams from Alabama, Tennessee, Florida, North Carolina, and Georgia came to compete on several different age levels.

Games began at the Memorial Auditorium and Textile Hall on six different courts from nine a.m. until around 11 p.m. for several days. I remember the tournament attracting over 200 teams, one year. Greenville was, indeed, the Textile center of the Southeast.

Each mill village had stars, some more recognizable than others. Many teams were formed just for the tournament and included college stars who were added to teams, in the Open Division and down. Some coaches would select players from different high schools, and they would compete together in the tournament. I played on a C team at Victor with players from Taylors High, Byrnes High and Greer High.

Each class of competition would add players to their rosters who would give them a better chance of winning. There were no rules regulating this other than age and that applied to the C Class only. Many players began their careers playing for the surrounding mill villages. Two recognizable names synonymous with the Southern Textile Basketball Tournament were Earl Wooten and Steve Brown.

When the Earl Came to Town

At the age of eleven, I saw Earl Wooten play for the first time. He visited the Victor YMCA with his Pelzer, S.C. Bears, the best team around in those days. When he crossed the center line, he entered his scoring range, with his deadly two-hand set shot. If you came too close guarding him, then he would drive around you and shoot his left-handed hook shot that he rarely missed, 20 feet from the basket. I became a big fan at an early age. When he did play at Victor, it was before a standing room only crowd. Before he ended his career, he would become legendary, throughout the south.

In 2006, I had the opportunity to interview Earl at his home in Williamston, S.C. We sat on his back steps and had a lengthy discussion. Earl was in poor health at the time and was receiving treatments for kidney disease.

Earl's eyes sparkled when he talked about his time playing basketball and baseball. The best basketball team on which he played was the Piedmont Rangers. Piedmont is a small town not far from Pelzer and, for years, hosted teams that dominated the Southern Textile Basketball Tournament.

Wooten laughed when he talked about fooling the referees during basketball games. If he was guarded too close, he had the habit of slapping his thigh with his hand while dribbling, and the "ref" closest to the play would call a foul on the player guarding him. "It worked almost every time," he said.

He signed a baseball contract with the Washington Senators and written into the contract was an agreement that he would not play any basketball off season. Earl signed the contract, but he continued to play basketball because he had such love for the game. Washington finally voided his contract, but he said he didn't mind that too much, because players weren't paid very well at that time.

Earl passed away about two months after our interview. It was a sad event for me, as he was the man after whom I modelled my own hook shot.

Steve Brown, the Pride of Victor

When you start listing players who made a lasting impact on the Southern Textile Basketball Tournament, then you would definitely add this guy to the list. Steve Brown played for teams from Victor, Greer Mill, Lyman and Daniel Construction. Brown was elected to the Southern Textile Basketball Tournament Hall of Fame, having won several All-Southern awards and serving on their board, as well.

A common denominator for the teams on which Brown played was that each team was a winner. The team that won the Class A Division in the 1970s, Daniel Construction, included several players from Greer. Wayne Gambrell, Steve Gambrell, Larry Gambrell, David Gambrell and Danny Gambrell represented their families and Greer well, having played at Greer Mill. The team also included David Dobson and Ronnie Long. Add those players to player-coach Steve Brown and you have a winner.

I'll have to admit to being a little partial when talking about Steve Brown, because he is a good friend with whom I spent a lot of time growing up, including times cutting a couple of cane poles, down by the creek that flows through Victor then fishing through the fence that surrounded the ponds behind Victor Mill, until the watchman would come around and run us off.

I also drove Steve and another fellow to the watershed, above Greer, one day, where fishing was illegal, and they were catching some good fish until a game warden came along. After the fine, they were the most expensive fish Steve ever caught.

I'm glad I was just the driver. Lastly, I believe he was the one to give me my first "church key," as it was called, and it wasn't used to unlock a place of worship. We still stay in touch with one another, after many, many years, and we met at the Y.

Fierce Competition

It was not unusual for the textile plants who sponsored teams to dip into the college ranks for players who participated in the tournament. Dick White, who grew up in Slater, S.C., and Harvey Tankersley, from Travelers Rest, played on the same C team, from Slater, in the tournament, and they were discussing which players each would guard. One said to the other, "You get the kid with the big eyes," who just happened to be Pistol Pete Maravich. Pete played on a team close to Clemson where he lived as his father was the coach of the Tigers then. Pete was only an eighth grader at the time.

Those guys were role models for others to emulate, just as Susan Jackson, Shelby Jean Brown and Joanne Stoddard were for the girls who played at Victor and Greer Mill.

The Athletic Directors Made a Difference

Greer Mill, Franklin, Apalache, Pelham, and Lyman were mill villages around Greer that turned out good athletes. Good athletic directors, like Tom Wilson, Punchy Howard, Fred Snoddy, Jim Cox, Wayne Godfrey and June Pruitt at Victor, Hal Huey at Greer Mill, Leon Gravley and Butch Miller at both Victor and Greer Mill are a few that come to mind. Willard Fowler was at both Monaghan and Victor, as athletic director and was a fierce competitor, as a basketball player and coach. Ralph Bogan, the athletic director at Apalache, invited me to participate in a summer baseball clinic. I credit him for teaching me how to hit and that was quite a chore.

There were also community coaches like Virgil Pruitt, who coached the Exchange Club, in baseball. Ott Durham and, later, Ted Lindsey, both coached the Greer City Boys, in football. All our athletic directors were men of high character and fine athletes. The boys and girls coming through the YMCAs were taught well.

The Victor Community Center, a white stucco building, which stood beside the Y, was a multi-purposed structure that housed a barber shop and social hall, which could be reserved for birthday parties and other functions. Rudy Godfrey, who had worked for Arthur Murray Studios, gave several people their first dance lesson, free of charge, in that building. After learning a step or two, boys would match up with girls and have a short dance or two.

Sewing lessons, birthday parties, church socials and many other social functions were held in the hall. J.P. Stevens & Co. also provided large bags of fruit, nuts, and candy for families, one for each family member, at Christmas. The boys who frequented the Y were expected to stuff the bags with the goodies. It was a fun affair.

J.P. Stevens & Co. wanted an all-inclusive environment for the employees. All sports had the best quality of uniforms and equipment with which to compete. So good, in fact, that when we played for Davenport Junior High and Greer High, we felt like our uniforms were a step down from what we had at Victor.

The Victor Company store had an abbreviated version of everything one might need. I bought my first baseball glove there, paying for it by the week, until the price of $6.00 was met. Tony Tipton, a good friend, and fine athlete loaned me his when he wasn't using it. It was a happy day when I got my first glove.

Two churches, Victor Methodist and Victor Baptist, were located at the beginning of the Victor community. Nearly every mill village in Greer, Spartanburg and Greenville had both a Baptist and Methodist Church. The south was, and still is, predominantly protestant.

Victor Elementary

Most students, I would guess, have a favorite teacher. In Victor I've heard Sarah Burch's name mentioned more than once, but especially by a friend, Frances Carpenter Southerland, who said that Sarah enrolled her entire second-grade class in the Junior Audubon Society, because of her love of birds. She apparently instilled in her students her love, as Frances is still an avid birdwatcher today.

Victor was known as a community where some tough guys lived, and they didn't always welcome outsiders. Walter Burch played for The Exchange Club in Little League baseball. Since they didn't have a field of their own, they were practicing at Victor. After practice and sitting alone beside the field, Walter was waiting for a ride when suddenly a few guys became suspicious and circled him, asking why he was hanging around Victor. Walt told them that he was waiting on his mom.

"Who is your mom?" they asked. He replied that it was Sarah Burch. They smiled and asked, "Well, why didn't you say so?" to Walter's relief. Victor welcomed outsiders but wanted to make sure they had good intentions.

A New Sheriff in Town

Mr. Mahaffey became principal of Victor Elementary as I entered the sixth grade. In a world where tall people seemed to rule, I wasn't selected as a school patrolman. They wore those neat yellow coats on rainy days, had a badge, and authority, as they stopped traffic and told students when they could cross. They were also on duty at recess.

While playing marbles at recess and wearing a pair of jeans that my mother had patched, another boy started poking fun at them. I tried to shrug it off but the guys around me gave me looks that were easy to read. *You're going to take that? He is insulting your mother.* That is forbidden. The fight began and I was escorted to the office by school patrolmen because I had delivered the first blow.

I was not looking forward to meeting the new principal. Sitting on a bench outside his office, the secretary kept giving me looks and smiling, interpreted by an 11-year-old as her saying, *Boy, are you going to get it.*

A tall, redheaded man opened the door and escorted me into his office, closing the door. He seated me and left the room, I assumed to get a giant paddle or strap.

He returned with two Coca-Colas, handed me one, and said, "Ok, tell me what happened." I went through every detail of the incident and then he instructed me on how to make better choices. He then pointed out that such incidents must have consequences. "What happens here must stay here," he added.

He then pulled out a strap and said, "Now every time I hit the desk with this strap, I want you to yell." I responded to his request and yelled five times as he hit the desk. He smiled and said, "Don't do it again." "Thank you, Lord, for Mr. Mahaffey," was my prayer that night.

I stayed in contact with Mr. Mahaffey through the years. He had his own musical group, Red Mahaffey's String Band, in which he played the piano at social functions, which included high school dances, and I always went by to talk. One day, after my graduation from Greer High, he offered me a Siamese kitten. I accepted, and the pet, whom I named Nero, became my constant companion at the University of Georgia.

When Baseball was King

Victor Mill Village, even in 1950, had what was called the "old side" and the "new side." Our home was located on the new side, beside the Old Woodruff Road, on Twenty-Second Street, which ended at the front gate of Victor Ballpark, later to become Stevens Field, the baseball center of Greer.

It was the home of the Victor Pirates, of the Western Carolina League, and the Victor Blues, a colored team, as it was referred to in 1951. It was also the home of John Ratteree Post 115 American Legion Baseball, which drew tremendous crowds, as the teams always went deep into the playoffs, one year finishing third in the nation.

When the teams weren't playing, the gates were locked, but it didn't stop boys from climbing the fences to have games of their own. You heard a crack, rather than a ping, of a bat, as you approached the park. Any broken, wooden bats were usually given to the batboy by the manager. A small nail or two and some tape was all a bat needed to make it usable again. Baseballs, which the teams fouled over the fence, at times, often made their way to someone's house, to be used as game balls for our pickup games.

The wooden grandstand, with its wire in front for protection, was the gathering place for a game that was easy to understand and loved by all. It was also a good place to take a date or to make friends with the opposite sex. Young people were decked out in their Bermuda shorts, a new craze. I bought a pair but only wore them a couple of times after Jeri Satterfield laughed at my skinny legs.

There was chatter on the field, a practice which, for some reason, was discarded somewhere along the way. Chatter was dialog, on the part of the players, for the pitchers and batters. "Come, Willie, come, baby, come, boy" might be the expression, accompanied by a whistle. It was a requirement for every kid, to know how to whistle. The sounds of the announcer were usually consistent: "That brings Mickey Strickland to the plate, with Murray Hall on deck, and Miller in the hole."

Ball chasers were given the responsibility of tracking down foul balls that flew over the fence. The problem was that he had some competition from young guys around the mill village who coveted the balls. It was on one such occasion that I caught one and began my journey home, with the ball chaser in hot pursuit. I felt the top of my head graze a clothesline, as I passed it, in O.E. Cline's yard. The ball chaser, who was about a head taller than I, wasn't so lucky, as I heard, from behind, the sound of the clothesline and a thump as he hit the ground making sounds as though he were being strangled. I felt so bad that I went back and helped him up, gave him the ball and apologized. I caught an angry stare the next day at the Y, as he was sporting a nice ring around his neck. It was a hazardous job.

Punchy Howard, the athletic director and manager of the Victor Pirates, finally decided that it was cheaper for them to make me their batboy, but one could safely bet that I would never apply for the job of ball chaser. Baseball was a big part of our lives and baseball players were our heroes, provoking arguments over favorite players and teams.

My favorite major league team was the Brooklyn Dodgers, and old friends Dan Harvey, Billy Vaughn, and I received many negative comments because we pulled for the Dodgers, as the South had no professional teams, although I always felt like my Victor Pirates could have competed with all of them. I may have been a little partial. All my senses come into focus as I recall those warm summer nights watching America's favorite sport.

Tank Hill

Tank Hill is actually a street that begins around 19th Street on Victor, crosses 18th Street, and ends on 17th Street, abruptly, if you happen to be riding a soapbox or a sled down a long, rather steep hill.

None of us had the funds to build an elaborate, well-designed soap box, which was a homemade vehicle that had four wheels, with two of them attached to a rod in the front, kind of like a baby buggy. A rod in the rear of the vehicle also had two wheels, attached to a wooden frame. A platform or seat held the driver, and some had a steering column rigged up, while others just had a rope attached to the front, which was a crude way of steering the vehicle, pulling it to the left or the right.

Victor had many backyard mechanics who were willing to offer advice on how to construct the vehicles, on the sly, because many moms did not approve. It was hard to get a girl involved, unless she was like my little sister, Linda, or Maxine Brown, who both were adventurous types.

The one important item missing from most soapboxes was a braking system. One relied on dragging a foot or taking a wide turn on Seventeenth Street, located at the bottom of the hill, which often resulted in throwing one from the vehicle. There was also the danger of a car approaching. A lookout was required to signal the driver of the soapbox to begin his journey.

One felt like the Wright brothers must have felt in Kitty Hawk (Kill Devil's Hill) when he or she made the first trip down Tank Hill. Some didn't apply their homemade brakes soon enough and wound up flying over the curb and into a large ravine.

Tank Hill ended where the Veteran's Park exists today. A broken bone or two and a few cuts and bruises were the worst side effects of such an adventure. My mother's remedy was to pour some pine oil into the cut, then tear a cloth and wrap it around the injury. Back out the door we went, as most who grew up on Victor were not pampered.

Snow or ice provided yet another adventure on Tank Hill for the kids in Victor. Since few could afford sleds, many homemade devices were used to slide on the frozen precipitation. Snow would provide a slower trip down the hill, with ice as the quickest and most dangerous.

Don Brown was having fun in the snow one day and was walking back up the hill, with one foot in Mr. Cunningham's yard to steady himself, dragging his sled behind him. He had almost made it to the top when Harold Allen gave him a little nudge, causing him to fall backward onto his sled, which initiated an unexpected, scary, backward journey down the hill. A screaming Don had no chance to slow the sled as it sped out of control, jumping the curb, with his life passing before him, and winding up in the brush at the bottom.

As he crawled out, he was steaming. He journeyed back up the hill to discuss the matter with Harold, who had wised up and was scampering toward home. Some great times, by all, were experienced on Tank Hill.

A Complete Community

As with most mill villages, Victor was somewhat self-sufficient, as it was intended to be, by its builders. The company store, Gaston's Dairy, and Dick Smith's Grocery would all deliver to our doorstep. Dry cleaners would also deliver, and medical doctors would make house calls.

We also had Bruce's Lunch and Harmon's restaurant nearby. Grady Bruce allowed us to hang out, as we didn't have much money to spend. Someone was always feeding the best jukebox in town, one that played great music.

Some played black artists, during a time when their music was not played on most radio stations of the day, unless you stayed up late at night. We listened to artists like B.B. King, Etta James and others, on a Memphis or Nashville station. Looking back, I think Grady probably prevented some juvenile delinquency by providing a place for us to gather.

What more could a person need? Mr. Phillip's Store, Miller's Café and Sam Godfrey, who sold hot dogs and hamburgers out of his home, as did Gene Cline. Champion's store was where I bought my bubble gum, which included baseball cards. Most of all, the people made the difference. Speaking to each other, as we passed one another's home, most were prone to sit on the front porch, in those days. Meeting friends at the Y, the ballpark, at Victor Baptist or Victor Methodist church.

We were a community that made it a point to know our neighbors and create friendships that would last forever. We were far from perfect, with a few that struggled in life after

Victor. I sadly watched, as a good friend was carried off to reform school. He was the most talented artist among us. Billy Vaughn, who went into the ministry, met with an old friend of ours before he died in prison after being convicted of murder. Life was challenging and sad, at times.

As I stare at the open field in that triangle, with the structures that no longer exist, the mill, the Y, the social hall, the Baptist and Methodist churches, the school, there are still the memories that no one can erase, the relationships that continue, even as we seem to vanish, one by one.

There are many faces that each of us can no longer gaze upon, some precious memories, and youthful experiences that are stored away that have become the most important images of my life. I suspect that you could pick any mill village in America and find people who still have pride in where they lived and a lifestyle that was like that in Victor.

Victor was a community within the city, and I felt, and still feel, a kinship with other mill villages. My friend Patricia Chambers lived almost her entire life at Victor and was finally encouraged to move, due to the new Inland Port Facility that would run by her home.

As I drive through the community today, it doesn't resemble the world in which we lived, but there are memories that make me smile. I'll always be a Victor boy.

LITTLE OLD GREER'S POST 115 GOES NATIONAL

Victor Ball Park, later to become Stevens Field, which was located at the end of 22nd Street, where I lived in the summer of 1957, was the perfect venue for American Legion Post 115's baseball team to display their skills, and they were very talented.

The ballpark had a nostalgic feel, without the neon lights one might find around some. Even the scoreboard was manned by a young boy who would hang a new number on a nail, when a run was scored.

The fence that encircled most of the outfield was wooden, braced in the middle with two-by- fours, horizontal to the ground, which gave the outfielder one last chance to climb it, and snag a ball before it disappeared into the night for a homerun.

The old grandstand, with the wire in front and located behind home plate, protected spectators from being struck by foul balls. It would remind one of old Wrigley Field, in Chicago. They are hard to find, these days and, even then, reflected earlier times.

The infield was dragged and brushed to a smoothness, designed to offer up no surprises for an infielder scooping a ball, unless of course a small rock may have been left behind on which a ball might ricochet and make an infielder, who was trying to field the ball, commit an error.

The pitcher's mound was smoothed off, as well, for safety measures. It would be the umpire's responsibility to brush off the home plate, which was accented with a lined batter's box on both sides of the plate.

A line defined a boundary down both first and third base lines and was extended, for both, to the fence, with a lined box for both the third and first base coaches to stand. Lime was used, in those days, to make the lines visible. On the outside of both base lines, temporary bleachers were added to accommodate the crowds gathered for the playoff games. So, the stage was set for an evening to watch what was, at that time, America's favorite sport. Some communities don't embrace baseball the way Greer did. Perhaps it came down to choices or that the love of the game just wasn't shared by the public.

The main competition for attendance in Greer, at that time, might have been one of three movie theaters and two drive-in theaters, or perhaps a nice swim at Chick Springs, Suttles Pool or Silver Lake, around Reidville. One could always hang out at one of the local drive-in restaurants, as well. Then there was always sitting on the front porch and waving, as the crowd shuffled past.

These other choices could be experienced at any time though and a Post 115 game was live, and you sensed that it was the place to be, as pretty young ladies would gather there, with their fresh summer tans and wearing Bermuda shorts, a new craze, along with bolt neck tops, of bright colors. Some in ponytailed hair, a fresh permanent or other new hairdo. Maybe a few were experimenting with a type of hair color, enhanced by the sun. Possibly, some were there to watch the game.

People seemed to sense that American Legion Post 115 was special that summer and the timing was perfect for a great season. In the summer of 1957, the people of Greer and surrounding areas were treated to some great entertainment by a group of young men who made baseball a fun game to watch, and there is no doubt that the team fed off the crowd, as the fan numbers increased with Post 115 winning most games.

American Legion baseball involved our best young talent from Greer but also good players from nearby schools, like Taylors, Byrnes, Blue Ridge and Travelers Rest.

Dudley Tollison was the first manager for the John Ratteree Post 115 American Legion Baseball Team, and he had some good teams of his own. His dedication and hard work had laid a foundation for success, but he eventually decided to turn the reigns over to Jesse Paul Edwards, who helped coach the team.

Knowing several of these guys, and if I had to use one word to describe them, then it would be "versatile". They had players who could play more than one position and perform well.

Donnie Dill, an excellent pitcher and hitter, who could also play outfield, also tended to hang out at my house, as he dated my sister, Linda. He also provided a strong bat. Dill, a Byrnes High graduate, and Billy Cooper, of Taylors, were talented hurlers whom opponents respected.

Dan Harvey was an outfielder who lived in Victor, on Snow Street, located by the park and making it handy for him to jump over the fence, and grab a fresh Greer peach that he had frozen over ice in the kitchen.

After graduation and his legion experience, Dan would go on to play baseball at Clemson. Paul Edwards moved Dan from the outfield to shortstop, to replace a hole left by Jack McKinney from the year before. Harvey grew into that position and flourished.

Greer had a plethora of young men who could fill the role as catchers in Ted Holtzclaw and Larry Johnson. Ralph Smith was another who saw some action behind the place. Larry Johnson would be the catcher on some nights but would also fill in at second base.

Ted Holtzclaw would play right field and was Greer's best power hitter. Don Lister, an old basketball teammate at Victor, was a good enough athlete to play anywhere, including catcher, but spent most of his time in the outfield.

Steve Brown, another Victor guy and a well-rounded athlete, played a steady third base and it was hard to get a ball by him.

Dicky Lanford, of Taylors, provided a good glove at second base and Lee Burns, of Travelers Rest, replaced Murray Hall, from the season before, and provided some clutch hitting at that position. Mike Smith, one of the younger players on the team, filled in at first base and had great potential. He was also a good hitter.

Morris Mason, another good utility player who hailed from Blue Ridge, was versatile enough to play different positions in the infield. Carl Leonard, with a foot injury, missed most of the season.

Jimmy Ayers, a young pitcher from Taylors, was destined to become a star of the future. Jerry Johnson, brother of Larry, was the youngest player on the team. The lefthander would be 2-0 for the season. A solid rotation of Lister, Holtzclaw, Mickey Strickland and Dill in the outfield rounded out a very strong lineup for Post 115.

Mickey Strickland was fun to watch at the plate, as a pure hitter. He also played a good centerfield and would soon sign up to play in the Los Angeles Dodgers' organization, making his hometown of Taylors proud.

Jimmy E. Howell was another pitcher who had some special moments during the season and would come through, in a timely fashion. He would eventually attend Presbyterian College, where he played baseball and basketball.

Many factors play in the success of any team. The team that preceded it was considered just as talented. Cohesiveness is a factor, for sure, and the timing in reaching one's peak for the season is important, as well.

The defense and pitching on the 1957 team were outstanding and, down the stretch, timely hitting would clear the bases, time and again. Playing good competition was also very important and they met local teams that would provide that while playing Inman, Spartanburg, and Woodruff. All three were formidable foes, with Woodruff becoming a heated rivalry.

Woodruff beat Greer twice in the early part of the season. An incident occurred when Don Lister was attempting to score from third base and the Woodruff catcher, Page, stood in his way at home plate. When the two players physically collided, I was sure that a bench clearing rhubarb was about to ensue. The tough competition Post 115 faced during the regular season would prepare them for the playoffs.

Greer, aided by some clutch hitting from Ted Holtzclaw swept Rock Hill and then a talented Greenwood team. Ted grew up in Franklin Mill Village.

He continued to pound the baseball against Garco of North Charleston, as Greer took the series four games to two, on the way to the Regional, which was to be held in Florence, South Carolina. Donnie Dill pitched a 4-hitter against Tuscaloosa, Alabama and Greer won the Region 5 Championship. Talented teams from Miami and Savannah were also eliminated.

The Sectional, which was held in Sumter, South Carolina, featured a couple of future major leaguers in Phil Gagliano and Tim McCarver, who both played with the Memphis, Tennessee team. Jackson, Mississippi was quickly eliminated in that series.

Memphis shut out Greer 9-0, but Greer went on to win the series in dramatic fashion with Jimmy E. Howell pitching perhaps his best game ever. He gave up only 2 hits on the way to a 5-4 victory over Memphis and was backed up with some great defense.

Years later Dan Harvey and Steve Brown were at a Braves game in Atlanta, when the St. Louis Cardinals came to town, with McCarver as their catcher. Tim came out of the dugout to recall the old contest between Greer and Memphis, in the Sumter series and he wanted to know the name of that pitcher whose pitch had a tremendous drop at the plate. McCarver went on to have an illustrious career as a major league player and sportscaster.

"Little Old Greer" became a favorite expression of the announcers in Billings, Montana, where the national playoff was held. Greer faced Cincinnati, Ohio, Portland, Oregon, and Washington, D.C. They finished third, with a season record of 32-7, and pushed the competition to the limit.

We all huddled around our radios and listened intently, and pulled for those guys who made us so proud. The memories, the call by the crowd for the team to rally, pandemonium as they did. It was one of Greer's finest moments, taking center stage, as the team that wasn't supposed to make it to the American Legion World Series, entertained America.

SCOUTING ADVENTURES WITH TOM WILSON

The Boy Scouts of America, as an organization, has experienced an unfavorable status in the last couple of years, attacked by the press and called upon to defend itself in the courts due to allegations of sexual abuse, which, if true, is an issue that should be resolved.

As a child I rarely heard the subject of sexual abuse discussed but I know it was a part of our lives. There have been civil lawsuits against leaders within the BSA organization, while some offenses are past the statute of limitations to prosecute, criminally, but others are still pending, as civil cases.

If you are to believe that people are basically good, then it is reasonable to assume that there are good people and good deeds associated with scouting. I was the recipient of both. Hidden beneath the lawsuits that have tainted the reputation of the BSA are some wonderful people associated with scouting and the performance of their contributions to the organization.

Troop 46, of the BSA, was in the community of Victor and met in a room in the rear of the Community Center. Golden L.

"Tom" Wilson, formerly the Victor YMCA Athletic Director, was our troop leader. Ken "Box" Godfrey was generous enough to donate his time, as well.

I had no ambition to climb to the rank of Eagle Scout. In fact, I never rose above the rank of Tenderfoot, even though I had fulfilled the requirements for promotion to second class. Tom Wilson tried, without success, to stir me toward the Court of Honor to receive the award but I was 11 years old, new to Victor and shy. I just wanted to hang out with the guys, keeping a low profile.

Tom's knowledge of arts and crafts was endless. One of my favorite activities was wood carving, since I grew up watching my grandfather, Boyd Bowman, carve walking canes. Carving wooden animals were my favorite objects that my grandad carved. Tom engaged us in wood carving.

Making bracelets and lanyards by weaving them with leather strings was another skill that I picked up from Tom. I made several and gave Fred Snoddy, our athletic director at Victor, a lanyard to wear around his neck to hold his whistle.

I seldom cook bacon today without thinking of Tom Wilson. That was my choice as an activity to earn the promotion to second class. My mom asked me if I needed help and I refused her offer, expressing the requirement by Tom to accomplish it on my own. I borrowed her black frying pan and built a fire in the backyard. When Tom asked me how it went, I told him that it was a disaster, that I burned it. He laughed and said that my fire was probably too hot. He was a firm believer in the discovery method if it did not endanger your life.

Life does not have to be complicated or expensive to be rewarding. Tom had us build a fire behind the Y and I attended my first wiener roast. My weight was under 100 pounds at the time, and I ate ten hot dogs, with my fellow scouts laughing.

The highlight of scouting was our trip to Camp Old Indian and then to the Great Smoky Mountains. T. L. Jones & Co. was kind enough to lend us a couple of coal trucks for transportation to and from both destinations.

At Camp Old Indian, we were housed in three-sided structures, called Adirondacks, with each equipped with three double bunkbeds. A group of ladies cooked our meals in a centrally located cafeteria and did a fine job in keeping a large number of scouts well fed, as we had troops there from many different cities.

We attempted to climb greased poles, studied artifacts, learned about Cherokee and Creek culture, had foot races, swam daily, learned to shoot bows and short sheet the guy next to you. We enjoyed all the activities.

Each of us were challenged to go down Old Slickum, a nearby sliding rock that was located by Poinsett Bridge, off Highway 25. We slid down the rock, into an icy pool at the bottom. Some mischievous Explorer scouts stirred up the sand, which acted as an abrasive to our rear ends after trips down the slope. As a result, we were all lined up to be painted on our raw butts with iodine at the end of our excursion.

We had a choice of hiking adventures we could choose from. One hike was to Saluda, while the other was a 10-mile trip across Glassy Mountain. The Explorer scouts hiked 25 miles across Hogback Mountain. While on the Glassy Mountain hike, Tom turned to us, put a finger to his lips, requesting silence, and motioned for us to backtrack, quietly. He passed the word that there was a skunk and that we would detour. We found out later that some local guys had their moonshine operation going.

The trip to Camp Old Indian was my first trip away from home for an extended length of time but the bonding effect with friends brought us closer together as a troop. It also helped me realize what a special leader we had in Tom Wilson.

A Trip to the Great Smoky Mountains

It is rare that a family on the mill village could afford to send a child on two trips, during a summer, due to the expense, but Tom found a way to make both affordable. The trip to Camp Old Indian cost 10 dollars for travel expenses, food, and lodging. The trip to the Smokies would cost six dollars for the week, and we would stay seven days.

There was a greater need for chaperones, and we had those in Bobby Bain, Roy Genobles, Leon Gravley, and Tom. They also had the responsibility of cooking each meal, although they did enlist a couple of Explorer scouts to help.

Riding on the back of a T.L. Jones coal truck was an adventure in itself. I tended to become nauseated while mountain riding in the back seat of a car, but the open air while riding on the back of a truck singing along with the troop and listening to their jokes and stories, was no problem at all.

We had a couple of rules to follow while camping. One rule was that there would be no eating inside of the tents, and it didn't take long to determine why, as a black bear came sniffing around our tents on several occasions.

Another rule was never to swim in the river without an adult present. The Oconaluftee River flowed through the campground. Tom didn't make too many rules, always adding that one should use common sense before acting.

My mother, who seemed to control the purse strings in our family, gave me two dollars to spend on whatever I chose to splurge on that week and another two dollars to spend on a pair of moccasins that were made at Qualla Manufacturing, which was Cherokee-owned and located on the reservation. It had no connection to the shops that were in the small town and that were predominately leased by others who were not part of the Eastern Band of Cherokee.

We made daily trips to the town of Cherokee, where we saw a couple of men standing in front of stores in full headdress. I was to learn that the Cherokee did not wear headdresses with lots of feathers. The Plains Indians did, but not the Cherokee. However, I discovered that visitors to Cherokee chose to have their pictures taken with chiefs who wore many feathers.

There was an older Cherokee gentleman who ran a small shop where I purchased a type of hard candy called jawbreakers. We befriended one another, and he always smiled when I entered. He invited me to shoot a bow one day, at a target he had set up behind the shop.

He did not wear a large headdress. In fact, he wore jeans and a shirt, but I could tell that he was a Native American. When I asked why he didn't wear the headdress like many others, he laughed and said that those people disgraced their culture by doing so. He did have long hair, worn in pigtails. He never charged me for shooting his bow and he seemed to enjoy my visits. I left there a better marksman, due to his lessons, and I also learned much more about the Eastern Band of Cherokee. I felt like I had gained a friend.

Unto these Hills, which is a historical drama presented in an amphitheater, made a lasting impression on us. As we left the production not many words were spoken. It was a powerful play about Cherokee history and the "Trail of Tears" which featured the government-forced-removal of the Cherokee and other tribes from their land, and their trip westward that cost thousands of lives. The outdoor drama left a few tears for us, as it was very emotional.

The trip to Gatlinburg, Tennessee was a diverting experience but reminded me of an oversized version of downtown Cherokee. I did enjoy watching the Venetian glass blower.

The most interesting event took place on the way into Gatlinburg. There was a young boy standing by the side of the road. His parents had apparently pulled over to watch a bear up close. They observed and laughed as the boy was poking the bear with a stick. It was upsetting to the bear, as any onlooker could tell, and a park ranger intervened very quickly, and when we left the scene, he was giving the parents an earful. Many people do not understand the strength and quickness of a bear, making it one of the most dangerous animals to roam the earth. Bear personalities are somewhat like dogs, with each having a different temperament and therefore unpredictable.

As usual, and as God surely planned it, the most unforgettable and priceless memories are provided by mother nature. Forget overpriced hotels, restaurants, and shops with their fake souvenirs and gadgets, which won't last past the trip home. Tom Wilson and his fireside chats stole the show.

After dinner we would gather around a fire, sometimes to hear a guest, but more often to have Tom share an adventure, his knowledge of terrestrial wonders, then, as we'd lie on our backs, he'd teach us lessons on the stars. He might then show us where the Southeastern Native American tribes were located and how they lived.

There were also his tall tales just before we returned to our tents for the night. My favorite was about 'Ringrangdoolia," a crazy person, who roamed the hills, strangling his victims and plucking their eyeballs out. Tom's last words were "and they say he is still up in those hills. Now you guys head back to your tents and get a good night's sleep." Of course, we would sleep with one eye open.

Tom invited Chief Standing Deer and his son, Paul, to the campfire one night to share the folklore of the Cherokee, and, as a bear passed through, the Chief commented that he was going to ride him. It apparently was a bear that the chief knew very well, and he didn't ride him, but he did pet him and walked along with him a few yards, with the bear responding in a friendly manner. We also had park rangers who joined us at the campfire.

Well, there are campfires and backfires. Leon Gravley had planned a practical joke one night, as he instructed two Explorer scouts to hide behind a Nash Rambler, which was located down the dark road that wound through the campground. The two scouts were to act as bears while the others, led by Leon, approached the designated spot. Unknowingly, a real bear was searching for food in a trash can behind the car. Leon shined a light in the bear's face, and it really upset the animal, as he suddenly stood on two legs and growled loud enough for the campground to hear.

A barefooted Jimmy Coleman, one of the scouts involved in the prank, stubbed his toe on the gravel road and pulled his large toenail almost off but still managed to sprint past all of us to escape an angry bear. His injury did require a visit to a doctor in Bryson City. Lesson for the day: Don't ever shine a light in a bear's face.

Years later, I spent a great amount of time with Frell Owl, who was Principal Chief of the Eastern Band of Cherokee. A project I was working on for graduate school was on the modern lifestyle of the Eastern Band of Cherokee. Frell invited me up to spend a few days to learn more about the tribe.

I was teaching at Gainesville High School at the time, and I asked permission to bring one of my classes up for a few days. He provided a ceremonial island, in the middle of the Oconaluftee River, as a camping area. I wanted my students to experience a little of what Tom Wilson had shared with me. We had Cherokee students join us around the campfire, friendships were made, and they shared their modern lifestyles with my students, as well as some of their heritage, not found in books, and of a local nature.

It was rewarding to spend time with my students in a setting other than a classroom, and the experiences at Cherokee altered my teaching methods. Frell brought artifacts for them to inspect, and he also educated my students about many preconceived notions that have been created, through the media, regarding the Cherokee.

What Tom Wilson shared with his Troop 46 scouts reached far beyond the 1950s. His teachings affected all his guys and their children. I certainly would never dismiss grievances brought forth against the Boy Scouts of America. If wrongs have been committed, then those responsible should be held accountable.

For all our young people not to enjoy the same opportunities that we experienced would be a grave injustice. We were fortunate to live during a time and in a place that produced such wonderful memories. We were also lucky to have been surrounded by such men of high character as well.

I can still see their faces, hear their voices, and feel their presence. No cell phones or any other technical devises, nothing man ever invented and produced, can replace what God put there for us to enjoy and no one presented it or took better care of it than Tom Wilson, a philosopher, a teacher, an artist, an adventurer, a father figure to some, and a man who was motivated by a sense of righteousness and love, where his boys were concerned. How could we have been so fortunate?

Troop 46

Front row (left to right): Keith Genoble, Hewitt, Reggie Cason Albert Sears, Tommy Holloway, Ken Wilson and Walter Monroe.

Second row (left to right): Bobby Vehorn, unknown, Jan Cline, Gary Jackson, Jimmy Coleman, Gary Holloway, Tommy Wilkinson, unknown

Back row (left to right): Ken "Box" Godfrey, unknown, Tony Tipton, Buddy Bowman, Doug Wilson, unknown, unknown, Tom Wilson

THE GYPSY CARNIVAL

There were two different types of carnivals that stopped in Greer during the 1950s. One featured entertainment like the Ferris wheel, the merry-go-round and several other rides. It attracted a large segment of the citizens and was allowed to set up on the Victor Elementary schoolyard. People from Greer welcomed this type of carnival as wholesome fun.

The other type was known locally as the Gypsy carnival and its owners were not allowed to set up within the city limits. Perhaps it was because of the nature of their business.

My mother, Ruby H. Bowman, forbade me from attending a Gypsy carnival. According to her, they existed for one reason and that was to cheat people out of their money. She also said that there were things there that I didn't need to see. Wasn't that enough reason to attend?

There were the fortune tellers, who used their crystal balls to share a glimpse into the future. Profound words may come your way, such as, "You will meet a stranger" or "Romance is in your future." That will be twenty-five cents, please. "Oh, and you will live a long life."

There was also an assortment of games, such as finding the pea under the shells, cutting the high card, or knocking the pins down with a ball, which was much harder than it looked and which few could accomplish.

A fence made of canvas surrounded the carnival. Its purpose was to keep out those who were underage. The age limit was 18 but the fence was very easy to crawl under and surely the proprietors didn't want to turn away any business, even 14-year-olds who were looking for some excitement.

The event of the evening was the strip show. We boys were less knowledgeable of the opposite sex in those days, I suspect, and misinformation was around to confuse a young man, as teenagers who were a year or two older claimed to know all there was to know about the subject. A dollar spent at a strip show broadened your education.

About the time the citizens around Greer were ready to complain about the carnival, their tents were broken down, packed away, and their caravan was heading out of town. The Gypsy carnivals seem to have vanished as a special kind of summer entertainment, and I suspect that the main reason was that local governments refused them permits.

That talk about the opposite sex with my father, that never happened, and programs like *Father Knows Best* on TV, did little to advance my education about the opposite sex, and I, along with the youth of Greer, S.C., would continue to rely on the discovery method, as the Gypsy carnivals finally faded away. I should have listened to my mother.

THE MAGIC OF MOVIES

Greer had three walk-in movies in 1952, the Grand Theater, located on Poinsett Street, the Greer Theater, on Main Street, and the Rialto, which was located on Trade Street, near the railroad tracks. Those three establishments managed to use up most of the money that I, as an 11-year-old, could muster in those days.

Fifty-two cents, my weekly allowance, was contingent upon staying in the good graces of my mother and completing my chores. If the mill was running and not curtailing one or more shifts, then times were good. If the mills started laying people off, then I sensed a nervousness around my parents. After experiencing the Great Depression not many years before they valued every cent they earned. I received no allowance during such times.

The *Greer Citizen*, our local paper, went to press once weekly and I stood in line to get my papers to sell, with my customers mapped out, if I could get to them before some other energetic young lad. The price for a *Greer Citizen* was 10 cents.

Money earned from selling them was what I considered my movie money.

If there was no money for entertainment then we relied upon discussions in our streetlight circle, which consisted of neighborhood kids who lived close by. Stretching the truth was the norm, while some of the kids became so addicted to lying that now, in their adult lives, they meet at a hot dog place called Rosie's for their storytelling fix.

It was during one of our sessions under the streetlight that the neighborhood rumor of a man with a hook for a hand was discussed. According to one of our older guys, the villain would molest and kill children. I shared this story with my sisters and warned them of the danger of going anywhere alone.

Fully informed, I allowed my sister Linda to join me for a movie one Wednesday afternoon. I remember the day of the week because we had received two free passes for a movie after attending fifteen straight Saturdays and having our cards punched each week. The passes were not valid for weekends.

We entered the theater, stopping first by the concession stand for popcorn, a Coke, and a pack of my favorite chocolate-covered raisins, with Linda always choosing her Malted Milk Balls. We had settled into our seats comfortably and were enjoying the coming attractions when a sound from a row back caught our attention. As we turned to look, a hook came to rest on the top of my seat. Coke and popcorn went airborne, as both Linda and I sprinted for the aisle.

The unfortunate soul who wore the hook was no doubt confused and perhaps humiliated by our behavior. I did manage to salvage some of my popcorn, and we watched the *Durango Kid* from back-row seats.

Billy Joe Allen and Mack Allen were my main movie friends and Saturdays would find us at Victor YMCA or at the movie theaters. It was the meeting place for school friends. Mack and I were at a Lash LaRue movie one Saturday and a man sitting two rows up from us was carving a popcorn box with his pocketknife. We were accustomed to watching older guys break out their pocketknives as many liked to find a stick of wood and whittle in those days.

An Apache was sneaking up on Lash, the main star. Suddenly, the whittler yelled, "Watch out Lash!!" to the amusement of others in the theater. He became the star of the show.

A special viewing of the classic *Quo Vadis* took place at the Grand Theater early one Saturday morning and I was told to return home after the movie. It was a long film and harsh for a sixth-grader. My teacher recommended it, since it was religious and historical, with the central theme being the persecution of Christians by the Romans.

The thought had already occurred to me that I could turn that Saturday into a movie-watching event. It is dangerous to turn a young guy loose with too much money and I had sold many papers that week. Exiting the Grand Theater after the showing of *Quo Vadis*, I decided to walk up to the Greer Theater just to see what was playing, and then make a major decision regarding the day's agenda.

A double feature! The Bowery Boys were in the first feature and Gary Cooper in *Dallas* for the second. There was no way I could refuse that. Gary Cooper was my favorite.

After leaving the Greer Theater and an enjoyable double feature I headed down Poinsett to Ponders for one of their delicious hotdogs, even though they were more widely known for their ice cream. As I passed the Grand Theater, I noticed that their Saturday double feature included two horror flicks. The first was *The Werewolf Man*, starring Lon Chaney, and the evening was concluded with Bela Lugosi's performance as *Dracula*.

As I munched on my southern-type hotdog with mustard, chili, and onions, I contemplated heading home, but I really did want to see the movies and I reasoned that my mother's punishment was already set, so I might as well make the best of my day. I watched the first feature and fell asleep toward the end of the second. Full of the day's munchies I slept until Dracula, I mean, the usher shook my shoulder and told me it was time to go home.

As I walked out of the theater, I was faced with darkness on my trip home. An 11-year-old boy's imagination was working overtime that night. There were several places on the trip home where a vampire could jump out from behind the hedges and bite a kid on the neck. He could also have his face disfigured by a hairy creature who needed a manicure and pedicure.

My walk became a jog and then a sprint as I made my quickest trip ever from town to Victor. I was met with a yelling, scolding, mother when I reached home. I looked at my dad and his silent, visual response back to me said that I was on my own. My last act before going to bed that night was to check the closet to make sure that no bats were hanging upside down, lurking in the dark.

Walter and Linwood Oliver, two brothers who lived a street over, asked me if I wanted to walk to the King Cotton Drive-in Theater one evening. We walked into the exit and sat next to a speaker and watched the movie. The people who owned the theater never bothered us, I guess because we always bought stuff from the concession stand. Teenagers tended to put a couple in the trunk of a vehicle and drive through the entrance. Kids 12 years old or younger were allowed to come in for no charge, if accompanied by an adult in a car.

The Greer Drive-in Theater and the Belmont Drive-in Theater were two other choices for the people to enjoy. Many teenagers, if they were lucky enough to have a date, didn't bother to watch the movie anyhow. There were many fogged-up windows around during the winter months.

Until 1952, when our first TV, an RCA Victor model, arrived at our home the movie theaters kept me entertained. Eventually higher prices at the concession stands and having televisions in homes affected attendance at movie theaters. In Greer, during the 1950s, we didn't have many choices, but movies were my favorite form of entertainment.

PUBERTY WAS NOT A PICNIC

I can't speak for the girls, but for me, as a boy, I was so leery and ignorant of what we would be facing as I entered Davenport Junior High School as a seventh-grader, that I walked softly, tentatively, wondering what changes I would be facing. The transition from our accustomed routine in elementary school was a little slow, due to the uncertainty of our next step in an unfamiliar environment. We knew a new pecking order would soon appear when kids from area elementary schools merged as one. We were faced with new procedures, teachers, and question marks about a principal we did not know.

One of the first unnerving, uncomfortable, and confounding changes was the wearing of a monkey suit, as we called it, during physical education classes. I wasn't fond of the excess room in the shorts, which were extremely brief, giving me the feeling that everyone was about to abruptly become acquainted with the private parts of my anatomy.

Each student, male or female, was required to purchase the necessary clothing for gym, which was my favorite class, excluding tumbling, a type of gymnastics exercise in which we cut flips on a mat. I almost broke my neck. The girls didn't care for their gym wear either, but I thought they looked much better in their one-piece outfits than we did in our blue shorts and white t-shirts.

Miss Seifert, who eventually became Mrs. Patrick, was my favorite teacher. She was not afraid to stray from the day's lesson if it would promote student involvement. We were reading the poem "Evangeline" and I commented that I thought it could be a movie. We then discussed which actors and actresses would be perfect for the main roles. At the end of the year, we had a dress-up dinner at the Wayside Inn. The girls wore nice dresses, and the guys wore white sport coats, with a pink carnation. The lady was full of ideas to make her class fun.

I liked the industrial arts class, also as known as shop, taught by Mr. Duncan, a very patient man. I made a tie rack and a lamp in his class and gave both to my mom. Music has always been almost as necessary in my life as food, water, and sleep. Nancy Myers had a class in music at Davenport, in addition to her classes at Greer High School, and I thoroughly enjoyed the class.

B.T. Gault, to me, was the ideal principal. First, it was quite evident that he liked kids. He was also hands-on, in that he was very visible, in the hall, at any place where school activities were taking place, and rarely in the office with his door closed. He was very positive and enthusiastic in his approach with students. He was also a fellow left-hander and very athletic, I noticed when he played first base for the Kiwanis Club in the city softball league.

I remember having a part in a play and how he encouraged me, even to the point of rehearsing my part, which was that of a preacher. He would make me repeat, time and again, the sermon given by the preacher, "and Elijah went like a whirlwind into heaven…" until he saw perfection. Most of all, I always knew that Mr. Gault genuinely cared.

When given the choice of playing basketball for the school team or the Victor YMCA team during my first year at Davenport, my allegiance was to Victor and I chose my neighborhood team. I did play my last year with the school team and had fun, except for a couple of games. Carey Smith, a friend and teammate, and I discussed our disbelief at how our coach, Mr. Taylor, could have scheduled not one but two games at Duncan Junior High during their sixth and final period of the day, in front of their entire student body. It was a humiliating experience because we had no fans. When we scored, there was silence, and loud cheers rattled the building when Duncan made a basket. We lost both games.

The good part of the gym class was being allowed to play sports, but the downside was having to get undressed to shower at the end of class. At that point the private part of your person had to be exposed unless you showered in your clothes. If one was further along in the development of his anatomy, then he was not overly concerned, while others might have been. At this point in our lives, body differences became significant and affected our self-image.

Then there was the issue of pubic hair. Some grew it earlier and it was embarrassing to those who didn't. I remember praying for more pubic hair and eventually being rewarded as we moved from the seventh to the eighth grade, but not before more pubescent embarrassment occurred.

Some of the girls were not far along in the development of their bodies either, so they may have gone through those years feeling inadequate as well. Girls matured earlier than the boys, so perhaps their dilemma was not as severe. Maybe that is why they seemed to go for the older, more mature guys and they dated them, once they got to high school. Some girls, perhaps the more mature ones, dated high school guys while they were still in junior high school. I just remember girls dating older guys.

Dating did not take place between junior high girls and boys as often during the 1950s. It was not unusual for a guy to hang out at a girl's house occasionally, perhaps sharing a swing on the front porch. We also met one another at birthday parties, athletic contests, church, or movie theaters. The Saint Valentine's Day boxes were still used in junior high and were a method to show the opposite sex that you cared. There was a pretty young lady named Joyce Williams that I had a crush on, and I bought her a card that was a little nicer than the ones I gave others, thinking that it would remain secret. When she received it, she made the fact public, with a yell, and I'm sure I turned several shades of red. Other boys gave me a hard time, because we were not accustomed to sharing our feelings.

Some eighth-graders obtained their driver's license at the age of 14, as did I, but I was not allowed to use it very often, so I rarely took a girl out in a car. Along with the problems associated with gym class, 13- and 14-year-old guys were also more prone to have acne and those who did were not very nice to gaze upon. The muscles had not yet begun developing well for some, and all the negatives that were piling up during that short period of time created low self-esteem.

Add all of that to my skinny legs and freckles to make me an unhappy camper. I didn't want to wear swimming trunks to Suttle's Swimming Pool, during the summer, for fear of having my skinny legs exposed. I also wore a hand-me-down swimsuit that did not fit.

My dreary world changed, somewhat, in my dark world of immaturity when I had one of those dreams, one night. You know, where you dream that something pleasant is happening, from which you definitely do not want to awaken. In fact, if the dream is interrupted, then an effort is made to dial it back up and keep turning the channels until it reappears. Yep, the dream in which you are on the threshold of manhood. I'm not sure if the girls had such dreams, I never asked. Like I said, there was still so much that I did not understand about them, and still don't, for that matter.

The Teenage Canteen

As a 12-year-old, I played on the Victor YMCA 115-pound Midget football team. That is, I practiced for three weeks, until an accident occurred the day before our first game. I was riding a bicycle through a redlight, located at Main and Poinsett streets, and was struck by a vehicle. I managed to escape with only a broken arm, but the accident destroyed me emotionally, because

I had put in so much practice time and was looking forward to our first game.

At season's end, an all-star team was selected from the four teams that made up our small league, which included Greer City, Apalache, Greer Mill and Victor. It was arranged that our boys would play a team from Shelby, N.C., which turned out to be their junior high team. Through Coach Fred Snoddy's generosity, I was allowed to travel with the team.

The league we competed in had a weight limit of 115 pounds, weighing in at the beginning of the fall. No player was allowed to gain over ten pounds during the season. Shelby's team had no weight or age limit, and I was surprised the field didn't tilt, due to their size, as they ran onto the field. Our guys looked at the coaches and asked, "We're playing these guys?" One of their players was over 200 pounds.

Billy Joe Allen was our quarterback, and he was constantly harassed by their defense. Our fullback, Jimmy A. Howell, remembers being hit by their defensive tackle, who weighed 230 pounds, and Jimmy was happy to have survived. The game turned out to be not quite as bad as expected, with a score of 20-0 in their favor, and thank God, no deaths, although there were a few bumps and bruises. There was a silver lining, however, when we were invited, after the game, to the Shelby Country Club, for a buffet and some entertainment.

Most of us were unfamiliar with country club settings, and I'll admit to being out of my comfort zone, as did a few others. We changed into some nicer clothing before attending, and we were graciously greeted and treated royally by the people staging the event. The food was great, music was playing, and there were several pretty girls in attendance.

The thought occurred to me that the girls were there as dance partners, since one of them strolled over and escorted one of our guys onto the dance floor after we had eaten. A young lady, perhaps a year or two older than me, walked across the floor and asked me to dance. I'd never danced before and explained that to her, but she said that she would teach me to slow dance, and I complied, despite my nervousness.

I found dancing to be exhilarating and I enjoyed my first experience. Besides, the young lady smelled much better than the guys I travelled with. The only good smelling stuff I'd ever worn was the hair tonic that the barber put on my hair at the end of a haircut. The banquet at Shelby did create, for me, some enthusiasm for dancing and I began to practice some steps with my sisters at home.

When it was announced that Davenport Junior High School would provide, for the students, a teenage canteen, where kids could go and dance, as well as play ping-pong, then I was on board. It turned out to be an interesting social experiment. The weekly event was held upstairs in the Paget Chevrolet building, where Gregory's, a boutique clothing store, is located today.

On that night, the boys might borrow a little of their father's Old Spice or Aqua Velva. My friend and next-door neighbor, Stanley Godfrey, had a pair of black pants with pink stripes down the side. He wore them with a pink shirt and some white loafers. I used a little Butch Wax to make my flattop hair stand up better.

As the small record player began to play either a 45 or 78 record, people were hesitant to mix socially, but the girls usually approached the dance floor first, sometimes dancing together. The crinolines, which were stiff petticoats worn by girls under a skirt or dress, made a brushing sound as they walked. Some wore as many as six or seven that formed a tent or parachute around them, or so it seemed.

Most of us were wallflowers, those who chose to hang out in a group, talking and too shy to mingle, unless it was music to which we could dance. Slow dancing was fun because we just moved our feet to no set pattern. Fast dancing was in a transition stage from "the Bop" to "the Shag," the latter being the new popular dance said to have originated around the South Carolina beaches. Ocean Drive Beach claims to be the home of beach music, which featured rhythm and blues.

Truman Henderson showed me some steps he had learned while taking dance lessons, but he was much, much better than I was on the dance floor. Most of us boys were just trying to survive without being embarrassed, but at home we grabbed a doorknob and practiced for the next event. With a doorknob, a partner was not required, but I discovered that it was much nicer to have a girl's hand. Those who did not participate in the fast or slow dancing would usually join in the square dances. After all, the person calling the dance instructed all dancers on which step was coming next.

Trauma was walking across the floor to ask a girl to dance only to be refused in front of your friends. I really did want to ask the girl who wore the zebra bathing suit to Suttles Pool the summer before, to dance, but fear of rejection left me flowering the wall. Conversely, I'm sure it was also traumatic for the girls when no one, especially their most desired dance partner, asked them to dance, since it was the boys who were supposed to ask.

The girls weren't afraid to dance with one another. The boys who were turned down had to swallow their pride and try again, aim lower or slink to a corner, vowing never to ask someone again. How did both sexes survive the trauma?

Miss Ellen Meadows, the girl's physical education teacher, and Coach Eddis Freeman, who volunteered from Greer High, were our chaperones, and tried to encourage socializing. With no price for admission, which many of us would not have had, and inexpensive refreshments, the Teenage Canteen became the place where young people from the city of Greer, Greer Mill, Franklin, Pleasant Grove, Fairview, Apalache, Pelham and Victor got to know one another socially. Some good memories.

The puberty years were not my favorites, and I don't believe I'd like to repeat them. I just wish I knew then what I know now—that I would live through them after all.

A FLIRTATION WITH JUVENILE DELINQUENCY

When James Dean was killed in a car accident in September of 1955, it affected teenagers in America greatly, including those of us in Greer.

I was attending Davenport Junior High School in Greer when his accident occurred, and when I told classmates that I had never heard of James Dean, they looked shocked, and I felt left out. I would, eventually, attend all three of the movies in which he starred.

The first time I heard the term juvenile delinquent was during the decade of the '50s. The movie, *Rebel Without a Cause*, starring James Dean and Natalie Wood, probably skyrocketed the sale of red windbreaker jackets, because many guys, suddenly, seemed to think they resembled James Dean.

Ruby Bowman, my mom, scolded me several times for drinking sweet milk straight from the bottle, just as James did in the movie. Young ladies in America also seemed to be affected by Dean, perhaps more than guys. In fact, my friend, Dee Clayton, hung his pictures all over her bedroom wall.

Blackboard Jungle was another movie that debuted in 1955, starring Glenn Ford and Sidney Portier. The movie's central theme was about juvenile delinquency in New York City. *Rebel Without a Cause* also dealt with teenagers experiencing problems in California. I guess you could say that some young people became preoccupied with juvenile delinquency. It became attractive to a few, perhaps.

As a freshman at Greer High, one day I was hanging out and listening to music at Jimmy A. Howell's house, which was located across the street from Davenport Junior High, when he brought up the subject of gangs. He informed me that he and a select few had formed a gang and asked if I would like to join. I was younger than others in the gang, but the idea seemed appealing, so I became a member of the "Black Raiders". I had to save my money to buy my own black tee shirt.

There wasn't much excitement or entertainment that would attract a teenager in Greer in those days, so any kind of action sounded appealing. A Halloween night was the first time that I met up with other members of the gang, which included Bill Groce, Don "Yankee" Addyman, Lum Edwards, and, of course, Jimmy A. Howell. I was the youngest member of the group, and I was to be initiated into the gang that night.

A night of reckoning occurred as we turned the corner of Line Street onto Cannon Avenue when it was decided that I would toss a small jar of green paint onto the porch of a house on the corner of Cannon Avenue. The jar of paint was handed to me, and I ran toward the house and threw it on the front porch, and we began sprinting up the street.

All of us had reached the opposite end of Cannon Avenue when we were stopped by Greer policemen, who lined us up, and started inspecting hands. Mine had the most evidence. We were soon in the back seat of patrol cars, riding toward the police department, located on Randall Street.

We were each given a chance to call home and then were held in a cell. At that point, I really did feel like a juvenile delinquent. My dad refused to come and sent one of my sisters, Sally Wilene, to the station. We were eventually driven to the vandalized house by policemen to meet Bob and Maggie Green, the owners. Maggie was very nice and understanding and told the policemen that she just wanted the paint cleaned up. I was sheepish, but sincere, when I asked her to please accept my apology.

The other boys and I cleaned the porch all night with cleaners until the wee hours. Later that day, my dad drove me back to their home, and we inspected the porch together. Dad was not satisfied with the results and we used paint to touch up the damage I had caused. Mrs. Green was satisfied.

A short time later, Jan Cline, a friend and teammate on Victor YMCA's Class D basketball team asked me to take in a movie after a game we had played. We went to his aunt's home to eat dinner first. We rounded the corner from Line Street onto Cannon Avenue and then entered the driveway of the first house.

We strolled through the front door and sat down in the dining room of her lovely, well-kept home and, after a blessing, we were asked to partake in a wonderful meal of meat and vegetables. Nervousness hindered my swallowing as I prayed that Mrs. Green wouldn't remember our last meeting, but she kept looking at me and smiling. Finally, she asked, "Haven't we met before?"

"Yes, ma'am," I replied. "It was on a Halloween night." She nodded, smiled, and then asked if I wanted seconds.

"No, ma'am," I answered. I then thought to myself that I'd already had seconds when I walked through her door. I never expected to return for dinner.

I received a hug from Maggie as I walked back out of her door, and she said that I was welcome in her home at any time. Riding past her home on many occasions, I've considered the decisions that could have been made concerning my actions that Halloween night. She must have been terrified and others would probably have dealt with me more severely. Perhaps if perpetrators considered their intended victims before an incident, there would be fewer crimes committed. We picked the kindest lady on earth as the target of our bad deed, and I knew that I would always regret my action that Halloween night.

Several juveniles around town were sent to reform schools during the 1950s. My flirtation with juvenile delinquency ended abruptly and I learned a lesson or two I've never forgotten. Jimmy A. Howell and I decided to become Marines instead. Bad deeds can come back to haunt.

SPEED TRAPS AND OTHER SURPRISES

In the early '70s, Ludowici, a small rural town in South Georgia, had a sign placed at the city limits by Governor Lester Maddox. It was placed to warn those that were about to travel through the town that it was a speed trap.

It would be nice if we could be warned ahead of time of the obstacles that affect us but, then again, it might affect our adventurous spirit and spoil the surprises we are to encounter.

Greer, in the late 1950s, had a couple of unexpected experiences for drivers. The method that was first used to check speed on the streets and highways was very obvious because a wire about the diameter of a garden hose was placed across the road. Line Street was the first place I saw the wire used and the street was appropriately named because not only was it used as the dividing line between Spartanburg and Greenville counties but also the speed device, at least part of it, looked like a line as it was stretched across the street.

Since there was no bush or tree for the officer to hide his vehicle behind, it eliminated any surprise, as the speed trap was completely visible. Then again, it reminded people to slow down, even if few traffic tickets were issued.

Toward town from where Bruce's Lunch was located on Line Street, a genuine surprise was offered up as vehicles crossed the Southern Railway tracks. Most local people knew to slow down almost to a complete stop due to the large dip located in the middle of the tracks, which ran north and south.

As I was having my two gallons of 29.9 cent gasoline pumped into my dad's '49 Chevy, the attendant at the Red Diamond service station said "You've got to see this." We both knew what was about to happen to the man driving a green Nash, who was obviously a stranger in town, speeding down Line Street toward the tracks, and I waved my arms for him to slow down.

It was painful to watch, but I'm sure more hurtful for him, because there were no seatbelts at that time. As his car lowered into the dip, at great speed, his head apparently hit something inside of the car, as he was bouncing around the vehicle, out of control. There was also a loud clinking sound as if something had broken. He exited the vehicle, holding his head, and we rushed to his aid, offering our assistance, but he seemed too mad and disgusted to be hurt. He did have to call a wrecker, however.

Greer didn't have the infrastructure in the '50s and '60s as it has today. The mills around town were curtailing operations and that meant fewer tax dollars for street repair and other improvements, locally.

By our only tennis courts in Greer, which at that time were located on Arlington Avenue, an extension of Line Street, a sign that warned of a dip in the street, was posted. The problem was that by the time a driver could read it, he was already experiencing an unsolicited adventure, which was compounded by the fact that a giant pothole amid the dip added to the fun. A sign should have been posted after the dip explaining what had just happened to the victim.

Duncan was the town of Police Chief Ertsberger, and it was not wise to go through his town speeding, because he would chase you to hell and back. When I was stopped by the chief for exceeding the speed limit one night, he ordered me to follow him back to the station, which I did. The chief and his wife lived in an apartment above the jail, and I was beginning to think that I would occupy one of the cells when he told me to follow him up the steps and into their apartment because he had left his ticket pad there.

As I waited for him to search, Mrs. Ertsberger and I began a good conversation. I had been very nice to the chief and had answered his questions with "Yes, sir" and "No, sir" responses and treated his wife with the same courtesy. When he came back into the room she said, "You shouldn't fine this young man." He said, "Well, since he has not done this before, I guess I could cut him some slack." The chief chose not to fine me. I thanked him and was on my way.

The skating rink was part of the chief's rounds, and we got to know one another pretty well. One day, as my sister Linda was skating, he asked me if I wanted to ride with him on his rounds, which would have been unheard of today, and I was glad to accompany him, since I was only hanging out until Linda had finished skating and flirting.

As we patrolled the area, he said that I would enjoy the next place, probably, because he had to police an area where dating teenagers liked to park. They would ride up into a nearby peach orchard, since there were several around in those days, and when the chief entered the area with lights flashing and the siren blasting, there was a mass exit of automobiles. We had a good laugh and I was happy not to have been one of them.

I had an opportunity to observe the softer side of the man who was considered by many considered to be one tough hombre, and ruled his little town with an iron fist. He really had some teddy bear qualities and was much kinder than his reputation presented.

Watch out for those speed traps, folks. You never know what is around the corner.

TALES OF A BAREFOOT RUNNER

My mother commented on it first, saying that I had what she called "running fits". The running fits would last throughout my life. I grew up with three sisters, two older and one younger who, collectively, created some contentious moments, even though I must claim responsibility for a few of those. Some people just cry or walk outside and scream but running always seemed to erase many of my frustrations. Sometimes we run to escape potential danger.

Having a curious nature can sometimes turn into disaster, especially when one wants to tear things apart. Some male adults like to tear car engines down, to better understand how they work. With a young boy it just might be a doll to tear down to discover what makes it cry. After my sis Sally Wilene discovered that I had taken the head of her doll off, looking inside of it, I was forced to make a quick exit, with her in pursuit. Sometimes we run to escape bodily harm. I found that running could bring sanity back into my life. There are also other reasons to run.

I had to learn the hard way not to believe all the advertising on the backs of comic books, with my desire to run faster. I believed that P.F. Flyers tennis shoes would enable me to run faster because, in an ad on the back of a comic book, it showed a person running with a jet stream coming out of the rear of the shoes. I was gullible enough to believe what the advertisement offered and was anxious to have a pair of the shoes.

I needed the shoes to play soccer in an apprentice league formed at Monaghan YMCA, in Greenville, S.C. My dad finally found a pair and they were the least expensive athletic shoes, costing around two dollars at the time, which was during the year 1948. When I laced them up on my feet, I was eager to try them out, so I ran down West Parker Road at full speed, but I didn't seem to be running faster. I came home as a dejected seven-year-old because I had expected better results. I shared the disappointment with my dad and granddad. My granddad replied, "Well, just make sure you don't sign up for the Charles Atlas Course they advertise, because you might be disappointed in that, as well."

From that point on, if I had to take part in a foot race, then my first move was to take off my shoes because I felt like I could run faster without them. My decision was accompanied by bee stings and "stumped toes," but that was just part of the experience.

I can even understand why the Greeks ran in the raw, although I was never tempted, except once, when I was almost caught skinny-dipping in a public swimming pool, after hours, with some guys one night. Some of the "streakers" I ran into in the 1970s may have had some Greek blood running through their veins, since the Greeks did run naked in the Olympics. Not sure if I'd want to go into battle under those conditions though. I was just content to run with my shoes off.

My mother had a designated time set, each year, when I was allowed to remove my shoes, and the date was May 1. Apparently, other moms set the same date, because I'd see kids running around and yelling, "May Day! May Day!" We even celebrated May Day at school and had our own Maypole and May Queen.

I wasn't running barefoot as a teenager the night Steve Brown asked me to help him get a Clemson rat hat that all Clemson freshmen had to wear. Brown had to have one for some kind of initiation at South Carolina, where he was on a basketball scholarship. I agreed to help him obtain one.

After snatching the hat from a guy's head one night at a high school football game, about a million Clemson students were chasing us and we were soon surrounded by them, when a couple of policemen intervened. The Clemson guy came forward to claim his hat and peace reigned once again.

Curt Hollifield and I did not take up running as a fad. We just loved to run. Freedom is gained as one runs. It feels as though demons are being purged. One day my dad dropped the two of us off at the Liberty Life building in Greenville and we ran back to Greer, in the grassy middle of the Super Highway, the only four-lane highway around.

We were past the railroad overpass and approaching the town of Taylors when a State Highway patrolman stopped us. "Boys," he said, "Ya'll can't be running down the highway like this." When Curt asked why, the officer explained that it was too dangerous.

"Well, our coach is not going to like this," replied Curt, "He is the one that told us to run."

"Who is your coach?" asked the patrolman. When we explained that it was Ralph Voyles, then I guess he knew the muscular man that was built as well as anyone in Greer. He said, "You boys be careful running." He then drove off.

Coach Voyles was seriously trying to build a track program at Greer High, and, although basketball and football were my favorite sports, I agreed to try out, running the 880 and the mile run. I also ran a leg in the mile relay and high-jumped.

I ran track barefooted at Greer High, even in meets. My feet were toughened from running without shoes and could even take the cinder tracks. Curt and I finished one and two, consistently, and it was always a close race, with him ahead in every race we ran together during the regular season, although there was an underclassman named Leonard Ponder not far behind me in every race. Eventually, Curt won his state championship, but not that year as he fell during practice and cut his leg, taking 18 stitches. He still managed second place that day in Columbia at the state track meet, running after having an injection of Novocain. The state track meet was the only race I ran with shoes in high school. I didn't perform very well.

We did have something to celebrate that day in Columbia, S.C. as good friend and teammate Jerry Nichols set a state record in the pole vault, a record that took years to break.

Curt Hollifield went on to win many other races and also received a scholarship to run track at Furman under legendary coach Chuck Rowe. He also came dangerously close to breaking the four-minute mile as he ran while stationed in the army, in Germany. I also ran my best mile while stationed at Parris Island.

We each run for our own reasons, but, in my opinion, preparing for life's obstacles is the most important of all. It is as if God is telling us to keep putting one foot in front of the other. You'll need it.

As I drive down Green Street in Gainesville, Ga. today, I see the runners out in full force, enjoying their runs, and I suddenly recall a time when people looked at Curt and me as if we were crazy. If so, then that rare breed seems to be growing. Just understand why you're running, folks.

THE TRACKS WE LEFT, CROSSED AND FOLLOWED

Sally Wilene Bowman, my sister, argued with me, at times, during our teen years, over the right to drive the family vehicle when it became available.

On one late summer afternoon, when we were too tired to debate the issue of who was to drive after working a long day at Taylor's peach shed for 50 cents per hour, I was the fateful designated driver. Peggy Brown sat in the middle and Wilene was riding by the passenger window as we began the journey home.

All day we'd been sweating in the open-air peach shed, in the humid atmosphere, with a fuzz permeated haze created as the peaches rolled down the conveyor belt past the glistening teenage graders and the dripping teenage ringers. The perspiration united with the fuzz to make all uncomfortable.

The three of us were tired and itchy, as we made our way down School Street in Greer, past the First Presbyterian Church and Central Elementary School, crossed the Piedmont & Northern (P&N) tracks and approached the Southern Railway tracks.

The track cut through a small hill, so the road went down a brief slope, crossed the track and went up a rise on the other side and you had to slow to a crawl as you went down and across. We were at the bottom of the dip when Wilene suddenly spoke my name. She didn't yell it, but I recognized the urgency in her voice as I quickly reacted, pulling the column shift down into low, causing the car to lurch violently forward across the track just milliseconds before the freight train sped past, missing us surely no more than a yard.

After the incident, I was stunned, in disbelief that I had placed us in near sudden death. Wilene applauded my reaction, after the fact, but as I released the clutch from shifting back into second gear, my leg began to shake so badly that I had to pull over, exit the vehicle and walk some, to regain the full use of my body.

To my knowledge, there were no speed limits on trains as they travelled through towns and cities, and they moved at a high rate of speed. There were no warning lights at this particular crossing either.

Trains striking vehicles occurred more frequently in the 1950s, due to a lack of caution signals, as well as the high speed of the locomotives. I was driving past the Paris, S.C., community when a train hit a car with several people inside the vehicle. I ran to the car, scattered down the tracks, to offer any help that I could. It was such a horrific scene that I choose not to describe it. There were no survivors.

My earliest memory of the Southern Railway is of a scene when I was four years of age. Virdell Beecham, Maude Beecham's son, held me on his shoulders as a passenger train passed very slowly. One of the cars carried a U.S. flag draped coffin. I was to find, at a later age, that the coffin contained Franklin D. Roosevelt's body, but I didn't realize the significance of what I witnessed. He had died on April 12, 1945. I lived on Seventh Street in the Victor community at the time, in a corner house beside the tracks.

The citizens of Greer lined the tracks in respect to the man whose voice entered our homes with his down to earth fireside chats on the radio. He was considered by many to be the champion who pulled us from the depths of the Great Depression, as well as the strong leader who would help us through World War II.

It was close to this time that two uniform dressed men were walking toward the front door of Mildred Clayton's home, not far from where she also watched Roosevelt's train come through. She was told that her husband, Vance, was lost in battle, during World War ll. At just 23 years old, she was faced with the reality that he would not be with her to raise their three children, Pat, DeLayne (Dee) and Michael.

Mildred was a tough lady, though, and bounced back because she knew she had to be there for her children, eventually marrying a fine man, Ed Cox, who had served in the war as a seaman on the *Lexington* and the *Hornet,* two of our major aircraft carriers during the war. They eventually had a child, a daughter, named Jan, who would complete the family.

If I had to choose a mother, other than my own, Ruby Hampton Bowman, then Mildred Cox would have been my choice. I was always welcomed into their home, and she referred to me as her other son. She passed away at the age of 96.

When someone lives to an age that surpasses so many, people say that she had a full life. This does not alleviate the pain, however, of those left behind. Mildred is missed by all and leaves a legacy of being a model mother to her children and will always be a heroine to all who knew and loved her.

Losing a family member was becoming far too common, as the war progressed. The train cars were loaded with service men headed north, to New York City, where they would be loaded onto one of Henry J. Kaiser's prefabricated "Liberty Ships," leaving for unknown destinations. More than 600 men from Spartanburg and Greenville counties died in World War ll.

Trackside Memories

A couple of hundred yards south of Seventh Street, in Victor, I was working, alone, for the R.P. Turner Co., unloading a train car filled with flour on the platform of warehouse number one, when Jimmy Hunt walked to the door of the train car with a distressed look on his face.

Jimmy told me that President John F. Kennedy had been shot. My reaction was "How bad?" He didn't know, but a short time later he returned and broke the news that our president was dead. I'm sure that nearly everyone, party affiliation aside, shared the emptiness, the sadness of that day, the shock and the tears of November 22, 1963.

John F. Kennedy was so charismatic that I don't remember another president holding the younger generation so spellbound. His speeches, delivered with a charming Massachusetts accent, captured audiences, and caused many to dream of becoming President of the United States.

I asked my younger sister, Linda, her choice for president, had she been old enough to vote and she said JFK. When I asked why, she replied that he was "so damned good-looking." I laughed, yet wondered how many other women would have voted for him for the same reason.

I received the news about John F. Kennedy only yards away from the depot where Lyndon B. Johnson came through, campaigning, when he ran on the ticket with Kennedy in the 1960 election. That spot was where Greer High seniors caught the train for Washington and New York, for their senior trip.

On that trip, some guys carried suitcases onto the train and the girls, in turn, brought food, since the dining car would not be open at night. I carried bags for Jerrie Ann Mathis, a good friend, and her mother had a dinner fit for a king, with fried chicken, sandwiches, and desserts that would have lasted for two days. Teenage guys are always hungry, and some had only one puny sandwich. We wound up having to share.

The P&N

The Piedmont & Northern Railways, more commonly known as the P&N, took longer reaching its destination, travelling much slower than trains on the Southern and making more stops. It catered to the towns and counties in the upper regions of S.C. and carried passengers, as well as freight.

Pat Sudduth, Bill Groce, Freddy Rowland, and Truman Tillotson were standing in front of Lewis' Drive-in one day, wondering what to do on a dull afternoon, when Bill spied a P&N freight car arriving. He soon had convinced the four of them that they should hitch a ride on the train and jumped upon a car.

The train was going to Spartanburg, but it was moving so slow that they could have walked the distance quicker. Bored from riding the slow-moving train, they hopped off before reaching Duncan, which was only five miles away, and walked back to Greer. A mile per hour was about their average since the train would stop and start repeatedly. I'm glad to have missed that trip.

I occasionally rode the P&N passenger train to Anderson, S.C., to see my grandmother. My mother paid the fare, which was less expensive than the fare on the Southern Railway, put me on the train and instructed the conductor where I was to get off. As an 11-year-old boy, I was independent and not afraid to travel alone.

At Anderson the train stopped outside of a pasture, which was located at the end of Redwood Avenue. I exited the train, walked across some wooden steps that straddled the barbed wire fencing that enclosed the pasture, then hiked across the open field that was home to some cows, and climbed over the fence on the opposite side. I then ambled up Redwood Avenue to my grandmother's house.

Most of my relatives lived in Anderson, and there were times when my parents' work schedule prevented them from carrying us to visit. The conductors on those trains were very reliable. One would come to my seat and inform me when my stop was coming. I'm convinced that we experienced more freedom at an early age in that trusting world during those years.

Many areas of the country have discontinued service on regional railroads, but the P&N lines are still being used for hauling freight.

The Perception of Tracks

Growing up in Greer, I heard the expression "the other side of the tracks," without thinking much about the implications of the phrase, or perhaps I was too young to grasp the meaning.

Gradually, it became clear to me that some regarded the tracks as a dividing line between the "haves" and "have nots," or the "city side" and the "mill side". There is little doubt that the perceptions of the neighborhoods were different, depending on where one lived.

At a young age, it is difficult to fathom the many advantages you have right before your eyes. When I was about 12, I walked by a large brick home located on the city side of Greer and realized that no such structure existed in the mill villages of Greer Mill, Franklin, Apalache, or Victor, but there are other considerations, when evaluating your quality of life.

When I attended Davenport Junior High School, *The Chronicle* was our school newspaper, of which I was the sports editor. One issue of the paper published some comments from students that were responses to the question, "If you had one wish, what would it be?" Billy Smith, a friend and schoolmate, responded by saying that his wish would be to live at Victor.

I teared up when I read the comment he had made, realizing that he loved Victor that much. He was to cross those tracks later, along with Don Lister, Steve Dillard and Mickey Stepp, to become my teammates on a Championship Victor Basketball D team.

My old friend and swimming buddy Jan Cline also played on that undefeated team and lived on Cannon Avenue and attended school at Victor. When we won the tournament, held at Woodside YMCA, Jan was named to the All-Southern Team and had his picture taken with Earl Wooten, a local sports legend. Cannon Avenue was always considered to be part of Victor.

I began, eventually, to appreciate what we had at Victor and at other mill villages, as well. Most had a YMCA, a ballpark, homes where we didn't lock our doors at night, and great people who looked out for one another. Gradually, we all seemed to gain some perspective of kids from other neighborhoods, the longer we stayed around one another. Sports, social events, and other activities around school remedied some of that.

Railroad tracks were such an integral part of our lives. They carried the dreams of other places, of adventures not yet experienced and penetrated our imaginations. In the age before we jumped on jets that carried us around the world, they were essential to our livelihood and helped build our infrastructure.

All industrial cities had railroads and today, with its inland port facilities in Greer, that replaced some of our old mill village homes, their roles are even more important.

Greer was built around its tracks. We made them, followed them, crossed them, and rallied around them.

MEMORIES OF OLD GREER HIGH

In the late 1950s, driving into Greer High School on North Main Street and into the parking lot in the rear of the school, with brakes squealing and horns honking, was a risk early in the morning, as students competed for preferred parking spots. Even some of the bus drivers were students.

If you lived within a radius of two miles from Greer High School, you were not allowed to ride the bus. Only students outside of the circle were permitted to ride. As a result, many walked to school if they didn't have a vehicle to drive. Since I lived inside the limit, according to school officials, I hitched a ride, occasionally, with the Forrester boys, down the street from our house, in Victor, one of four textile mill villages in Greer.

Most students entered the school walking by the agriculture room, which housed the Future Farmers of America and held classes for students interested in the subject, through the back entrance into a corridor, which led up to the classroom area on the first floor. The Greer High Band room adjoined the agriculture room.

As you entered the long hallway, the coaches' office was located on the left, where Phil Clark, Head Football Coach and Athletic Director, shared an office with assistants Eddis Freeman and Lewis Phillips.

As you walked on up the passageway, there was the gym on the left, where champions played throughout the 1950s. If the Yellow Jackets didn't become the South Carolina Class A Boys' Basketball Champions, then they made it to the finals the majority of the time. It was the most dynamic boys' basketball program around, considering the size of the school, during that decade.

As a young lad, I dreamed of someday playing for the Greer High Yellow Jackets. Greer High's basketball population came from different sections of the town with a select few players coming together as one, if they were fortunate enough to make the cut, as the competition to make the team was stiff.

The Greer High gym was also the site for our "sock hops," which were held after the games. Students were required to remove their shoes before dancing on the gym floor, to music played on a phonograph. Admission was free.

Directly opposite the gym was the boy's dressing room. It had a section for physical education and another for whatever sport was in season to the right, as one entered, where teams had their dressing room.

Next door to the boys' dressing room was the girls' dressing room and across the hall was an office for the girls' physical education teacher and girls' basketball coach. Betty Weir used it and later, Coach Bobbie Dellinger, who became the girls' basketball coach after Coach Lewis Phillips began coaching the varsity boys.

Twenty-eight cents could purchase a school lunch in the cafeteria, which was located next up the hall. If you didn't have the money for lunch, then perhaps you might have enough for a couple of three-cent cartons of milk.

The lunchroom ladies made great yeast rolls, which were free. Honey and/or sorghum syrup was kept on the tables as well, so there was no reason to go hungry. Some students, like Sondra Edwards Massengale, would forego the school lunch, occasionally, so that she could have the ice cream, sold in small cartons and eaten with a wooden spoon.

The cafeteria, at times, had tables stacked in the corners and was used for dances, such as the Christmas Ball, the Freshman Frolics, the Sophomore Hop, and the Homecoming Dance.

My former principal at Victor Elementary kept his band ready to play for some of the dances. His group was called Red Mahaffey's String Band. Most of the music was slow, with songs such as "Picnic" and "Moonglow." Occasionally the band would play a tango or a rhumba, and those who had mastered ballroom dancing could now showcase their skills. Coats and ties for boys and nice dresses for girls were usually recommended for those occasions but all students were allowed, regardless of dress. B.L. Frick, the Greer high principal, welcomed all at the door.

(The Junior-Senior Dance was held off campus, at times in the Armory, near downtown, or in the Gold Room of the Jack Tar Poinsett Hotel in Greenville. Other venues were used, as well. The Gold Room at the Jack Tar Poinsett featured a circling chandelier that gave off its reflections on the ceiling, a pleasing effect, that added something special to the dance. Guys who invited a date to the dance would usually rent a tuxedo or dinner jacket, as few owned one. It was customary to present a corsage to the girl he was taking. The Junior-Senior was a long affair, as a couple usually dined at some dinner club afterward.)

Across from the cafeteria was a door leading out to the commons area, where kids gathered to talk during lunch time. The flagpole was there. After lunch, many would congregate in this area, on a nice day, and socialize.

One of my favorite teachers, Mr. Marvin Collins, occupied the next room up the corridor, where the subject was Industrial Arts. Mr. Collins was a paratrooper during World War ll. He jumped out over France on D-Day and landed in a tree, surrounded by thick fog, so dense in fact, that he couldn't see the ground. He was afraid to move for fear of making noise, with the enemy nearby. Collins dangled from a limb for hours, until daylight approached, and the fog began to clear. It was at that point that he realized that his feet were only about six feet from the ground. He was a great storyteller.

Hazing

Hazing was prevalent at Greer High School during the 1950s. An incident was usually laughed off unless someone was injured. Although I was a target of the seniors and other upperclassmen just like other freshmen boys, I took it in stride, as initiations were expected.

There was a freshman in the middle of his shower during a physical education class, when four upperclassmen ushered him to a towel cart, which had wheels. He was thrown into the cart, his body covered with soap suds from the shower and partially by the towels within the cart. He was then rolled to the upper part of the corridor, just as the school day ended and left there, as students rushed down the corridor toward the parking lot.

Fortunately, a couple of classmates came to his rescue. They could identify with his misfortune, as they were targets also, and he was rolled to safety, but not before other students had a good laugh. If you objected too much, it made matters worse, so we just smiled and accepted our fate, up to a point.

Seniors also had their fun at the flagpole during lunch. They targeted all freshman boys. I was chased, on several occasions, and felt very fortunate that there were no distance runners in the crowd. We ran around the building, through the parking lot, by a cannery, and through the nearby cemetery.

By the time we had finished that run, we all had to return to school to avoid being tardy for class. I went without lunch, when necessary, unless I ate on the run, as the routine continued. The girls were targets for pranks, as well. I was coming out of the gym one day when someone pushed a girl out of the girls' dressing room into the hall in her slip and held the door handle so she couldn't get back through the door, leaving her screaming, in frustration.

The tradition of running a guy's pants up the flagpole, a year-to-year custom, finally ended when Mr. Maxwell, our assistant principal, decided to restore order, especially during lunch. There were four guys, all seniors, who were truly responsible for removing a freshman's trousers one day, during my sophomore year. They were taken to his office and asked if there were others involved and they began naming names.

The public address system was busy that day, as around 70 names, all guys, were called, even though only the four were guilty. My name, along with many other innocent bystanders, were called to the office. It was decided that we all would be punished, and we were given a choice, being expelled for two weeks from school or accepting 100 licks, to be administered by coaches, in increments of 10 a day. Corporal punishment was still in effect for disciplinary indiscretions for all grades in Greer's schools. Nearly all of us chose the licks.

For a paddle, Coach Clark had an archery bow that was sawed in half. Coaches took turns in administering the licks. As I reflect on the pranks that took place, the punishments that accompanied them, and other incidents that were a part of our daily lives, I wonder how many lawsuits would have grown out of those incidents today. Some pranks would continue at Greer High. I heard of some boys releasing some chickens in the library as late as the 1960s.

Somehow, we survived the ordeals, and eventually much of the hazing that took place seemed to decrease. Today, and those days in the 1950s, were vastly different. I don't feel scared, but I'm confident that there were a few who did.

Parades, Snake Dances and Bonfires

The homecoming parade usually began by taking the same route all parades took through town, beginning down Poinsett, and veering right, down Trade Street. Each senior football player asked a girl to sponsor him. The car carrying her might have some advertising from the provider of the car, and if it was a local car dealership, then the parade provided some good advertising.

The high school band, of course, would march in the parade and, unfortunately, sometimes their efforts to stay in step were jeopardized with little boy peashooters lining the route.

A few school club floats were included, some class officers, cheerleaders and class sponsors, or girls who represented each class. The Greer High football team and the Greer High band also had a sponsor, voted on by each, to represent them.

All of those being honored would sit on top of the backseats of the convertibles, for all to admire their freshly prepped hair from a visit to a salon the day before or, perhaps, even the day of the event. Whatever the effort put forth, the parade-goers, in respectably large numbers, were the recipients of their efforts, as they rode down Trade Street, waving as they passed. Some may have made a special trip to Alta Cunningham's, a fine ladies' clothing store, to get that new outfit out of "layaway," a term not used very often these days.

The night before homecoming there was a special pep rally around a large fire, made up of donated wooden objects and scrap wood. The students would gather in a field near the school. The band played, speeches were heard, and the cheerleaders led us in cheers. The Snake Dance ended the affair, as we all joined hands and, in motion, would wind around the fire. Viewed from above, it would resemble a snake, slithering. The pep rally would end with the singing of our alma mater. Teachers, coaches, and others would supervise the affair and make sure that the fire was extinguished.

A high school football game during our time, especially homecoming, was the best show in town on a Friday night, and the dance afterward was icing on the cake.

The Age of the Beauty Queens

Through thorough examination, I'm not sure how beauty pageants came into existence, but Greer seemed to have quite a few during the 1950s.

The success of Miss Universe, Miss America, Miss South Carolina, and Miss Greer pageants trickled down to the high school level. It seems that for every major dance held we had a beauty queen presiding, and I never disagreed with that, although I didn't always agree with the choice.

Sometimes beauty stood in the corner. It may have been that girl who didn't have the wardrobe, the makeup, and enough popularity to influence her to compete. These were the ones who might have gotten off the sideline, came to the 20th class reunion and were quickly noticed by guys who asked, "Who is that beautiful lady?" Her confidence and self-esteem grew and perhaps her financial independence rose to the point where she could afford those accessories that highlighted her beauty.

A girl can't blame those who did compete, either. When we consider the plight of a young lady of the 1950s, not many choices existed. If she played athletics, she ran the risk of being called a tomboy. If she evaded social activities, concentrating on academics, then she might be accused of being a bookworm. If she pursued guys, as guys pursued girls, then she was frowned upon as a girl of questionable character.

Girls did not wear long pants to school, even though they did wear rolled up jeans with bobby socks, for leisure activities. In the 1950s they wore long skirts or dresses, which covered the knees. Miniskirts had not evolved, and Helen Gurley Brown, and other women of influence, had not yet made their mark.

In the adult world, men held nearly all executive positions because they were considered to be the head of the family and the provider. If one happened to be a single mom, then too bad, she deserved her status. The fact that it was a man who helped her become a single mom didn't seem to matter. This is, at least in part, the mentality of the 1950s in small Southern towns, and it was passed down from adults to adolescents.

Becoming a beauty queen, at any high school function, was an honor and one of the few chances for a young lady to have her place in the sun.

My Favorite Beauty Queen as a Freshman

Please don't feel offended if my selection of certain favorites doesn't coincide with yours. Greer High School, in the 1950s, was blessed with many beautiful girls who could have been selected as class beauties, homecoming queens, and sponsors for our football players. That your choice for any of these categories would differ from mine is possible. There was no homecoming for other sports. Besides, as a freshman, I was in awe of the senior girls, who were at their peak with their physical features and loveliness.

In September of 1956, I was in a mad rush to get to my first-period class on the bottom floor of Greer High on my first day of school. I was dodging the senior boys who had their class rings on with the stone turned down, so it would hurt more when they struck freshman boys on the head.

Ninth-Grade Algebra scared me more than the senior boys. I was not looking forward to entering the classroom, and I was about there when I saw her. As she strolled down the hall, it was as if everyone and everything else vanished but her. I was mesmerized by her presence, her lively walk and her energy, her beauty and elegance, so much, in fact, that right before we met in the hall, I ran into a set of lockers as she looked in my direction with a smile. She laughed at my perceived slapstick move, but it was truly an accident and unintentional.

I asked, "Who was that?" The guy standing next to me informed me that she was Lorita Miller. I had heard Sally Wilene, my sis, speak of her on several occasions, since both were seniors and good friends, but I was not prepared for that moment in time. Freshmen guys could become infatuated by older girls, but reality brought us back down to earth.

What would impress me most about Lorita was that I never remember her passing me anywhere without an acknowledgment, as well as that smile. Glory and fame affected some upperclassmen, who became popular at school, but it didn't seem to affect her. That image still remains for me. She was, indeed, my favorite beauty queen at homecoming, and appropriately, honored during halftime of a game played by perhaps the greatest football team that Greer High ever fielded, the eventually undefeated Yellow Jackets of 1956. It was only fitting, in my opinion, that she was the one chosen to represent her school as our homecoming queen that year.

Lorita Miller at Homecoming in 1956

A Team for the Ages

The 1955 Greer High football team had a great season, with only one loss, but Spartanburg High School spoiled our season with a 20-13 victory over the Yellow Jackets. Greer High had a very good quarterback in Steve Satterfield, who continued his career by becoming quarterback for the South Carolina Gamecocks, and they also had an All-State senior center named Butch Miller, who was chosen to play in the Shrine Bowl, the annual football game between North Carolina and South Carolina.

Having lost all-star Satterfield, there was a question mark at quarterback in the season of 1956, and the top candidate for the job was a senior named Bobby Gravley. Some felt like he was too small, weighing only about 125 pounds. I had seen him play for Victor and I knew he was capable.

Sometimes it is not just the size or athleticism of a quarterback but the chemistry that is created when he steps into the huddle. Bobby was tough, believed in himself and took charge of the full house T formation that Coach Phil Clark ran. The T replaced the single wing offense that Greer had previously run, without a QB under center.

The belly option was the meat and potatoes of the T formation and Bobby ran it to perfection, with two very capable halfbacks in Murray Hall and Joel Hendrix, and a freshman fullback named Bobby (Booly) Duncan. Billy Gregory and Jimmy A. Howell were other backs used frequently.

Gravley was not afraid to stand in the pocket to pass, although Coach Clark ran a lot of bootleg passes to get him on the corner where he could see the receivers better. He had a couple of good ends in Jack McKinney and Lonnie Harley, and Murray Hall was a weapon as well catching the ball out of the backfield.

Greer returned some very good linemen from the 1955 season. The Howard boys, Bobby and Billy, held down the left side of the line, while Hugh Granade and David Boozer were on the right. Bill Grant and Charlie Brank alternated at center.

The 1956 team played a tough schedule and defeated all opposition, winning against a strong North Charleston team 13-9 and a good Columbia High team by a score of 33-0. The Gaffney High School Indians were always a strong foe and Greer shut them out, 19-0. They also blanked Spartanburg, 26-0, the team that had spoiled their season the year before. The Clinton High Red Devils played Greer the closest, with Greer winning 19-16.

As there was no playoff system in the 1950s, Greer High, after surviving a tough schedule against good competition, some games against larger schools, the consensus was, among sportswriters and football coaches, that Greer High was the best South Carolina high school football team of 1956.

Murray Hall, a Star of the 1950s

Murray Hall became the most recognizable running back in the South, and colleges as far away as the Big Ten Conference sought his services. The elusive back, who did not possess Olympic-caliber swiftness but had good speed, could dazzle with his quick moves and an ability to wiggle out of close situations. He was Greer High's best weapon and the school's participant in the Shrine Bowl, where he was named the Most Valuable Player. He was also MVP in the North-South Game, which featured the northern section of the state of South Carolina playing the lowland area, covering Columbia to the coast.

Murray went on to win many other awards and was named as a Wigwam Wiseman All-American. He was a good athlete in all sports and eventually signed a baseball contract with the Chicago Cubs.

A lasting impression that I have of Murray is of his unselfishness. As a younger guy, who looked up to him, he would talk to me during batting practice before Legion games and toss me his first baseman's mitt, as we were both lefthanded, when he went to bat. He would then hit some scorchers down the first base line to see if I could catch them and laugh when he got one by me. To me, he was the real "natural".

Murray Hall and friends on Senior Trip to NYC

Greer High Basketball

There has never been another decade in Greer High's history that has seen the success of the Greer High boys' basketball teams of the 1950s.

The Class of 1953-54 came close to a state championship, making it to the finals in Coach Eddis Freeman's debut as Greer High boys basketball coach.

The Class of 1954-55 brought the boys' Yellow Jackets a state championship with a very talented team. Although the girls' team came up short of a state title, Susan Jackson and Florence Cameron distinguished themselves as good players.

The 1955-56 Greer High boys' team was special. Not only did they win the State Championship in their classification but, at the end of the season, they played the best team from South Carolina's highest classification and defeated Charleston's Bishop England High School by a score of 74-70, giving Greer the right to call themselves the state's best. It also gave Coach Eddis Freeman his second straight state championship.

The 1956-57 boys team made it to the finals but lost, as did the 1957-58 team, which lost in overtime in the finals, giving Eddis Freeman four teams to make it to the state finals.

Steve Brown of the Class of 1957-58 was the most prolific scorer of the 1950s, averaging over 25 points a game one season. Brown would go on to win the Most Valuable Player Award in the North South All-Star Game. He would also earn a basketball scholarship from the University of South Carolina.

During the run for the State Championship in 1958-59, I witnessed the most amazing comeback that I've ever seen in a high school basketball game. Greer High was trailing Lancaster High by 20 points at the end of the third quarter.

Coach Lewis Phillips used a full court press to make the game closer. Pat Sudduth was not usually depended upon for scoring a bunch of points but time and again his steals helped bring the Yellow Jackets back. Greer High gained 31 points on Lancaster in the fourth quarter to win by 11, and then advanced to the state finals. When I later became a basketball coach, myself, I would use that game as a model, time and again, to illustrate what can happen when a team finds itself far behind.

Greer High went on to win the State Championship by defeating Orangeburg for the state title, behind the solid play of Steve Foster, Don Lister, Jan Cline, and Wayne Gambrell.

Greer High girls who played basketball during the 1950s also distinguished themselves with good play, winning a couple of district titles with stars like Pat Gowan, Brenda Garren, Ann Dobson, Carolyn Reeves, and JoAnn Stoddard.

All these teams, players, and coaches brought pride to the city of Greer.

Clubs and Extracurricular Activities

Fortunately, Greer High did have an abundance of clubs and other extracurricular activities in which to participate, most of which included both males and females. Aside from student government activities, there were over 20 clubs. A few were restricted, as members had to be voted in but there were many in which anyone could become a member.

Music has always been my escape. If life in high school was not going well, I was known to skip a class, without permission, and migrate to the music room to join Betty Hunt, my choral music teacher, and sing my frustrations away. It was a world where I felt comfortable and where my bad experiences in a math class were pushed aside. Music remains my passion.

Greer High had an excellent music department that displayed great talent, such as the beautiful voice of Frances Payne and the soft, wonderful sound of Tommy Edwards, as well as the excellent piano playing of Don Hunnicutt, eventually a concert pianist.

I don't remember any student being turned away from participating in choral music, although the Greer High a cappella choir, the Greer High boy's quartet, and the Greer High girl's sextet were selected from those trying out. The mixed chorus and girl's chorus provided a chance for all to participate. Tryouts for musicals were also held.

I was a member of the Greer High quartet, which featured four-part harmony, like a barbershop quartet. I had the opportunity to perform with two Victor friends, Tony Tipton and Billy Vaughn. We began singing together in the Victor Boys Choir, which represented Victor Elementary School. Our Greer High School Quartet, with some different members each year, performed at many functions around Greer.

We went out to the county prison and sang for the inmates one Sunday morning after having performed at the Cotton Club, which was a local dinner club, the night before. The prisoners at the county farm came up afterward and gave us each a homemade billfold, and they really made us feel appreciated. It was a good experience for all.

The Greer High band was our pride and joy, representing us at games, concerts, and parades. We had several students who later played in college and university bands. The Greer High band was invited to participate in many out-of-town events, maintained a high standard of excellence, and brought honor to Greer High.

The music department and athletics were the two main interests that kept me in school. For my younger sister, Linda, it was basketball and band, where she played her drums. I was willing to go to classes to participate in athletics and music, up to a point. We all had our own private world in which we functioned best and there we entered our comfort zones. It was in those settings that we found common bonds with others and where friendships were formed.

I've always believed that extracurricular activities play an important role in the overall success of students. A socialization occurs among students with a common interest and is reinforced as acceptance within a group occurs. It is an opportunity for you to find success through participation, and with that success, a reason to come to school. It is what you enjoy the most.

The more emotional, intuitive, and creative student might prefer the arts and English over math and science, but they will work hard in those classes in which they are weaker to achieve desired goals. Some educators have referred to extracurricular as "the hook" that gets students who struggle with certain subjects to school and keeps them there to achieve overall success. Good teachers also keep students in school.

Fronde Rice, the Teacher

As I suffered from insomnia, I tended to keep late hours at night listening to long-range radio stations while lying in bed. Stations from Cincinnati and Memphis had good rhythm and blues.

Early on a Monday morning of my junior year, the lack of sleep was wearing on me, soon after being seated in Fronde's English class, and I quickly dozed off. No one fell asleep in Miss Fronde Rice's class.

While I was sleeping, Miss Rice pinned a flower in my hair and, at the end of class, had students tiptoe out of the room. As the next period's class tiptoed in, she seated them quietly. She also had notified the teacher of my next period's class, across the hall, what was taking place. All of this occurred without my knowledge, as I was in deep slumber.

I awakened about midway through second period and looked around at a class I didn't recognize, amidst their laughter. I gathered my books and walked out of her class, apologizing for my error, and she just smiled. I then had to suffer the humiliation of entering my next class, as students enjoyed themselves, at my expense. I never went to sleep in Miss Rice's class again.

Miss Rice was a lady who had fun with the incident, and she also was a master teacher. I never worked harder in anyone's class, and she was very stern and disciplined in her approach to students. The steady diet of writing and learning new vocabulary words took more time in her class than all my other classes combined.

Essays and themes were returned promptly graded and with comments and suggestions throughout. Fronde prepared me for college better than any other teacher. Her icy stare, when she felt like we were not concentrating as we should, would grab a student's attention quickly. No time was to be wasted in her class.

After graduating from Greer High School, I was going through Marine Corps basic training at Parris Island. We had a drill instructor named Bischof, who resembled a grizzly bear. A recruit remarked that the sergeant was the meanest SOB he'd ever met and asked if I agreed. I laughed and replied that I had an English teacher named Fronde Rice who could chew him up and spit him out.

She was the best teacher I had at Greer High, although another young teacher named Linda Stevens was in her rookie year at GHS, and was becoming very popular with the students.

A Hero Reemerges

It was during my sophomore year at Greer High that life became difficult. I was discouraged in my math class. Students were asked to go to the chalkboard, occasionally, and solve an equation and that practice caused me to dread walking into the room.

Students process at different paces and mine was slower than the norm. Many others were quicker and ready to move on to the next step. Slower students are reluctant to raise their hand to ask a teacher to repeat a step because they don't want to appear dumb. Sometimes they are faced with a choice. Raise your hand and ask for clarification or waste the remainder of the class sitting in the fog. I chose the latter.

Basketball was over for that year, and I didn't have much to look forward to. I began cutting school and not showing up for classes at all. I was tempted to ask my parents to sign papers for me to enter the Marine Corps and had actually talked to recruiters.

Late in the school year, when I had missed too many days to complete my sophomore year, Coach Lewis Phillips pulled up in front of my house. He had missed seeing me around school and had been told that I was considering a different alternative, other than attending school. We sat in a swing on our front porch and talked for close to two hours. Coach was always a good listener.

In our conversation he convinced me that quitting was not an option. That once I began that practice then it would become second nature to do so again. He then began to lay out a plan.

First, it was suggested that I attend summer school. Secondly, he wanted me to come out for the varsity basketball team, even though I would not be eligible to participate in games during the fall semester, although I could practice. Finally, he made me feel secure in the fact that he would be there when I encountered problems during the school year.

I had Mrs. Pugh that summer for algebra and I learned more in her class than in all math classes combined during the regular school year. She suggested that I complete my homework in the morning before school, since my class was at ten am. She shook her head over the fact that solving polynomials came easier, for me, than binomials. She was a very patient lady and I believe that she helped me turn the corner in math. Geometry came easy with Doc Maxwell, who was also very patient. I was still classified as a sophomore, due to not having any credits the last semester of my sophomore year.

I tried out and won a spot on the Greer High varsity basketball team, practiced with the team, and was allowed to play in games after Christmas. Until that time arrived, Coach Phillips tracked my steps, both in and out of the classroom. He also asked me to ride with him on trips to scout football games for next week's varsity opponent. During those trips, we had some good talks and I'm sure it afforded him an opportunity to check on my progress. Taking a half year off from school meant spending an extra year at Greer High School. That year gave me time to reflect on what I wanted to do with my life.

Throughout that year, Coach Phillips was not only my coach but a supporter and friend. I believe a bond was created when he was my principal at Jordan Elementary and he continued it at Greer High. Sally Wilene shared the same bond with Coach Phillips, as she played for him when he coached the Greer High varsity girls' basketball team. Sally was a tough act to follow at Greer High. She was a member of the National Honor Society, top ten percent of her class and the recipient of a scholastic scholarship to Winthrop College.

As seniors, Dennis G. Lynn, a good friend and I were asked to go to Coach Phillips' farm and do some work, helping to clear some land. We earned money to go toward our senior trip. Another time, during my senior year, Coach Phillips asked me if I would write, organize, and direct a womanless wedding and he paid me $25.00 for the effort. It soon became clear to me that he was doing all that he could to make my life have some meaning during that school year. The athletic department put on the wedding, with Jimmy Few as the groom and Dennis Lynn as the bride. It turned out to be a fun affair.

When later I decided, after serving in the military, that I wanted to teach and coach, I knew that I wanted to be just like the man at Greer High and, earlier, at Jordan Elementary, my mentor, Lewis M. Phillips.

I began to realize that he was also a mentor to others, like Dennis. I understood that I could not be Lewis Phillips, that his concern for his players, beyond time spent on the court, was what made him special. Imitating another person did not seem a wise move, so becoming the best me became my goal.

Dennis would also become a coach, working with Willie Varner, at Woodruff High, and Eddis Freeman, at Hillcrest High School. Eventually, he would enter the ministry.

There was one thing that I did for my basketball teams that Coach Phillips did for us. I never could play the piano like Coach Phillips, but I had many of my teams come to my home to eat and sing Christmas carols. When your coach invites you into his home, it is special.

A good memory was when the basketball team went to Coach Phillips' home in the Jordan community and we were told that we each had to eat five hamburgers. I had no problem with that. We then fellowshipped together, as a team, celebrating

Christmas, only about 200 yards from the little house in which we lived when I went to school at Jordan.

It dawned on me one day, after having taught and coached for many years, that the former students and players who returned to visit me were mostly those with whom I had spent time in sports and other activities past the normal school day. We saw each other in a different setting, and we had more one-on-one time together. In short, we knew one another better.

We all want our independence but there are times when we need one another to conquer life's struggles. We need those angels in our lives, who watch over us and I've had a few. I look out back and watch my redbirds on cold, wintry days. I wonder, at times, which one is Coach Phillips.

In Retrospect of Old Greer High

For me, one of the greatest legacies of Old Greer High was that it afforded me the way to overcome my self-doubt. When I reflect on those Greer High days, I remember tumultuous times and special times, romances that never came to fruition, lessons learned, sometimes the hard way, and missed opportunities. I learned that inhibitions can roadblock success. I also learned that we all have weaknesses and strengths. We love to do what we can do well. I loved my music, but I never considered it for a career. With my shortcomings in math, I found my strengths in other subjects. I am thankful for the memories and friendships that flourished, that now seem to become more precious by the day. Go Yellow Jackets!

THE RALPH VOYLES WAY

In the Greer High yearbook, Le Flambeau, many accolades appeared under the name and picture of Ralph Voyles: a multi-honored lineman on the football team. co-captain and captain his junior year and senior year, respectively, the team's MVP, and Greer High's representative in the S.C. - N.C Shrine Bowl his senior year.

What is most telling about Ralph's high school career is the number of different activities in which he was involved, such as serving as class president three different years. He was in several clubs, and was the stage manager for the Junior Play and the Senior Play. In short, he was involved in much more than football. He was also an excellent student. I found his strongest attribute to be his heart, his concern, and feeling for others.

Newberry College awarded Ralph a scholarship in football, where he excelled in the sport and academics. Upon graduation, he began fulfilling his obligation to Uncle Sam, serving a two-year hitch in the U.S. Army.

Suddenly, Ralph appeared back on Greer High's doorstep, not as a god, in my perception, but as a man who'd come to serve. He reminds me of the main character of the TV sitcom *Welcome Back, Kotter,* the teacher of a class of loafers known as the Sweat Hogs. And in fact, I belonged to that group.

Voyles' reputation grew as a man devoted to his students. I've heard many good athletes, including Greer High's own football All-American, Steve Greer, who played for Coach Voyles, testify to that fact. All of us who were on teams that he coached were challenged and pushed hard and became better players by having him as our coach, a coach who demanded our all, and to whom we wanted to give our best for him.

Being a team player was what good athletes strive to be. That is the right way, the Ralph Voyles way. I suspect that my then basketball coach, Lewis Phillips, whispered something in his ear that someone who was walking a thin line was heading his way because I felt the structure he provided, personally, as a track coach.

Physical Education was less structured in the 1950s. We would exercise and then play basketball, volleyball, or softball outside during the spring. Coach Voyles would allow me to go down to the track and run during my first period class. When I was loosened, he would start the stop watch then keep an eye on the guys playing softball, and still be able to yell my time on intervals as I ran the mile. I fulfilled the requirement for the Physical Education class, and this allowed me more time to study in the afternoon.

If students in Physical Education class started to fight, then breaking out the boxing gloves was a way to settle the argument.

Coach Voyles gave four guys one boxing glove each when they began to push and shove during a half-court basketball game.

He then blindfolded each one and turned him around several times so that he would have to locate the others. It was a funny scene, as the class stood on the side of the court, laughing, with the boys swinging at air and connecting rarely. It was an interesting way to disarm an incident, but it worked. Even the participants enjoyed themselves.

As a distance runner, Coach Voyles milked every bit of effort out of me that spring. I trained hard most of the time, but it was difficult, as an athlete who was undisciplined in his lifestyle, as I was known to sip a beer and smoke a cigarette occasionally, and I did not sleep long at night, as I kept late hours. He never gave up on me, or any of us. The afterthought, years later, was that Coach Voyles provided what many refer to today as the right culture. He believed in his athletes and delighted in helping them set their goals and achieve them.

During my senior year at Greer High, Coach Voyles picked the coldest night of the winter, and then he invited several athletes/students to join him on a campout at Paris Mountain, when the temperature was six degrees Fahrenheit. We kept the fire stoked, roasting wieners and marshmallows. It is during such moments that I began to appreciate him as a man, and not just as a coach. He could have picked other occupations that would have earned him far more income. Surely, he looked within for the answers because I could tell that he enjoyed his work.

Coach Voyles ended his coaching career as the defensive line coach at Wofford College. In recent times, Coach Voyles has taken on yet another mentoring role, that of a grandfather. I met him at Rosie's Hotdog Restaurant one day, and he introduced me to his grandson, whose handshake already resembles a vice, just like his grandfather's.

This, then, is the legacy of Ralph Voyles, teaching young men to live by the rule: "Do the right thing and maintain the right perspective." He is a man who was led by his heart, who knew when to take the spotlight off himself and nourish the development of others, and who always had the love and respect of those around him.

Steve Greer "All-American at the University of Georgia"
– Coached by Coach Voyles

THE KNOTHOLE CLUB

One of my favorite activities is attending college football games, especially on a crisp, fall afternoon. Sometimes, when I was a child, my dad and I would attend a Clemson College game together.

We would drive by Hinton's in Greenville and pick up a couple of their famous "footlong hot dogs" to munch on riding to Clemson. My friends Billy Joe Allen and Mack Allen might be tagging along for a couple of those games.

I'm not sure when "tailgating" became such a popular event but in the 1950s it wasn't as popular as it is today. There are some folks now who don't even leave the tailgate to attend the game, watching it on their televisions that they have rigged up at the site, with enough food to feed half of the fans.

When we arrived at the stadium, Dad would go through the general admission gate, paying around $1.50. I would be admitted through the "Knothole Club" gate for 50 cents. This was before the madness began. Today one must make a half-zillion dollar contribution just for the right to purchase a season ticket, the amount depending on the location of the seats and how long you have been purchasing season tickets.

IPTAY at one time meant "I pay ten a year," that is, 10 dollars a year for a basic membership. Each major university has its own plan. I'm not sure what one pays to join IPTAY now.

Frank Howard was the coach at Clemson at the time, and he was running a platoon system with his teams. Eleven guys would enter the game and play both offense and defense. "Unit One" would start the game and then "Unit Two," with another eleven players, would relieve the first unit. Sometimes, the second unit would outplay the first.

I remember one of Howard's teams having two quarterbacks from the same town, Greenwood, S.C. Harvey White was the quarterback for the first unit and Lowndes Schingler led the second unit.

There were times when people criticized Frank Howard's offense, referring to it as "Three yards and a cloud of dust." I enjoyed watching the old Tigers play. Clemson didn't win a national championship then, but Howard-coached teams did compete well and were usually winners.

Well, the Knothole Club is gone, and it is now the spot where the Tigers run down the hill and touch a rock before going out on the playing field. It is sad that there is no longer a spot for the kids who cannot afford the price of a ticket, to squeeze in and watch a game on a Saturday afternoon.

As for people who second-guessed Frank Howard's offense. That hasn't changed much. They're just criticizing others now, all over the nation. People can use their computers to pull up "Hudl." "Hudl" teaches wannabes to learn different offenses and defenses coaches run, and the fans can now become better than any coach. A guy can learn the jargon and instantly become coach of the year, telling the coaches what they should do, from the stands. They can't teach a kid to pass, run, kick, block, or tackle, but hey, they know the important stuff, just ask them.

The week of "Big Thursday," when folks could attend the State Fair and take in the Clemson-Carolina game, was a big affair. I always enjoyed the arguments among fans, even more than the game. It really was a rivalry in those days.

I don't remember people dressing up like they do today at college games, wearing their schools' colors, especially students spraying their bodies with paint. My dad wore his overalls, with his hat cocked to one side and I'd sport my Wrangler jeans, which were rolled up, of course, as most of us wore them that way. You didn't have to worry about the length of the jeans when you bought them, just the waist size.

If you were to sit still in "Death Valley," the popular name for Clemson's football stadium, you could probably feel the spirits of old Clemson stars like Buck George, the great running back of the 1950s, who was also a chief of the Catawba Nation.

You may also feel the spirit of my old friend Ray Sanderson, who didn't drive at the time and talked me into taking him to games at Clemson on occasion. Ray's world consisted mainly of working at Victor Mill, delivering a paper route early in the morning, and, for a while, living in a room over the Wayside Inn in Greer, S.C.

His leisure time was spent at Victor YMCA, as sports, all kinds, centered his world. He was a big St. Louis Cardinal fan, loved his Clemson games, the Greer High Yellow Jackets, and the Victor Pirates, not necessarily in that order.

At times, upon greeting me, instead of calling me by name, he would jump into his role as a sports announcer, saying something like, "Steve Foster steps to the free throw line, with this game tied, he looks at the rim and delivers...he made it, folks!! With ice water in his veins, he won this game by one point against Spartanburg!" Then he may strut around with his arms in the air.

When I took Ray to games at Clemson, I'd have to wait after the game for Ray to go shake hands with Frank Howard, congratulating him on a win or consoling him if Clemson lost. He also loved to meet sports personalities, and I watched him shake hands with coaches, Wally Butts of Georgia, Shug Jordan of Auburn and Paul "Bear" Bryant of Alabama, when their teams played at Clemson.

Ray, like my father, has since moved on and both may be sitting around and listening to one of Frank Howard's jokes somewhere, but people who are dear to our hearts are the ones who give us the special memories. We love them and miss them but there are times when an episode will leave us warm and with a smile on our face, and OK, a tear might appear, as we remember those moments together.

There was a time when one did not sit at home looking for the channel on which a team's game would be televised. We just leisurely strolled into the stadium, with those we loved, and enjoyed an afternoon of football.

Life consists of such memories we relive, time and again, and I have a few special ones, which become even more so, with the passage of time.

BOOTLEG WHISKEY, HOT RODS AND MUSIC

The mountain people in Appalachia have a unique lifestyle and are wonderful people, even though books and movies have not always treated them as such.

Homer Carlisle Campbell, also known as H.C., or more often referred to as Carlie, was born several generations after the Whiskey Rebellion, but the art of making good corn liquor, which many referred to as moonshine, was passed on to him. His family can trace their roots back to clans in Scotland, several of whom wound up in Appalachia, around the Blue Ridge mountains. Several Campbells live around Gowensville, S.C., which is about 14 miles from Greer.

Carlie served his country in World War II and was to be shipped out to the Pacific when he learned that his wife, Verle, was having problems delivering their first child, Dixie. He was refused liberty to go home to check on her, but he was not to be denied and went home without permission. He wound up spending a few days in the brig for the incident. Carlie was then sent to North Africa and eventually to Italy. He was also decorated for his service.

Carlie's eyes glistened as he shared, with me, some of his bootlegging experiences, as he was known as a person who took great pride in the making of his spirits, an art that not many, if any, could equal. As an employee for R.P. Turner & Company, wholesale food distributors who were in Greer during the early 1960s, I remember placing bags of sugar and quart and pint jars on the back of pickup trucks, or in the trunks of cars, on several occasions. The company was, after all, selling legal products.

There were more ingredients, of course, that went into the making of whiskey but every location that produced it had to have the availability of water. Moonshine production had long been established and was thriving in the 1940s and '50s.

The *revenuers* were those people who were charged with the responsibility of regulating the laws associated with the manufacture and sale of alcoholic beverages. The general attitude towards the federal agents, who destroyed the liquor stills of bootleggers, was less than favorable by the public, who believed they were already paying too much money in taxes, even though the task of enforcing the laws overlapped the jurisdiction of other law enforcement agencies.

It was very rare that someone snitched on bootleggers, since they could be your own neighbors, friends, or members of your church. Besides, someone might want a jar or two of their own, for medicinal purposes, of course. It is the main ingredient in some good cough syrup, and I was told by one doctor that it was the alcohol that held the most value. My parents made cough syrup with whiskey and rock candy. My mother and dad declared our home to be dry, otherwise.

Carlie had to work hard to find places that were concealed enough to make his whiskey, even though there were plenty of isolated spots between Greer and the mountains. Agents would walk up beside the creeks and the rivers because bootleggers needed water. Sentries were posted to watch for them.

Recalling a man who was assigned a sentry post and decided to take a nap, Carlie told how he placed a wasp on his lip, which brought a quick reaction, as a reminder to stay awake. With agents walking up and down the rivers and the creeks, looking for signs, he finally decided that it made more sense to just dig a well and make his whiskey beside it. Many people preferred the home brew to the liquor store's variety of booze.

Carlie Campbell in his race car

Hauling Moonshine Was No Picnic

Delivering illegally made whiskey, aka *White Lightning*, to one's customers, posed another risk, because law enforcement officers were always on the lookout for violators. Creativity could breed success and Carlie Campbell was on top of his game. Fast cars that cornered well were required for mountain roads. He was a skilled driver, spending time competing on the dirt racetracks around South Carolina.

Ed Mabry was a likable S.C. Highway officer who was a friend of my father. We lived on Highway 14 in the Jordan community in 1951, and Ed would always wave when passing. I remember him pulling my father over once just to talk. Years later, Ed was known to give chase to Carlie, who proved hard to catch, in his fast '39 Ford with a Cadillac engine that was taken out of an ambulance in Gainesville, Ga.

A car that was jacked up in the rear raised eyebrows because it was viewed as a bootlegger's car. Placing a load in the trunk of the car made it look normal. Carlie was known to remove the back seat of his vehicle, replace it with cases of moonshine, covered with a blanket, and have Dixie, his daughter, and Steve, his son, sit on them. His car never had a raised rear.

Carlie's moonshine days are in the past, after finally giving it up, concentrating on selling automobiles. It seems that he was successful with every venture, no matter what the challenge. For a while, he averaged selling about a car per day. My sister Sally Wilene knew him well at the time, and described him as a handsome man, with a great personality.

Carlie was part of a subculture in the South, as more people decided to supplement their income by making illegal spirits. There was one house, within the city limits of Greer, that had booze running through a faucet.

The movie *Thunder Road*, which was filmed around Western North Carolina, romanticized the illegal alcohol industry, and starred Robert Mitchum, a popular actor of the era, and Keely Smith. The film popularized bootlegging even more, especially the fast cars, equipped with certain gadgets, which were added to evade capture by law enforcement officials.

The bootleg liquor industry, despite law enforcement efforts to eliminate it, would continue to thrive in the south. There were enough stills and people involved to keep federal agents busy.

The Machines We Admired

Many people frequented the movies and teenagers had hopes of driving their own dream cars. The automobiles in the movies were fast and innovative, equipped with devices used to give them an edge on their competition in road racing. Fast cars were already popular all over the country and the movie industry hyped the practice of building fast engines.

It was not unusual to witness a raised vehicle hood at some restaurants, like Lewis' Drive-in, around Greer, to show people their high-powered engines, the addition of a four-barrel carburetor, or perhaps three deuces, a racing cam, a fuel injection system, or anything that would increase speed in a short distance, as was the case in drag racing.

Most of the drag racing was done on the highways, in the wee hours of the morning, until Greer built its own drag strip, which didn't completely stop road racing. Word spread quickly when a couple of fast cars were about to go head-to-head, and crowds would gather to witness the event.

It wasn't just in Greer that hotrods flourished, but in cities all over America. Hot-rodding had arrived on the local scene. The desire for speedy vehicles even popularized NASCAR racing in places like Darlington, S.C., and Daytona Beach, Fla.

Like many others, I could not afford a fast machine, because it was expensive, and I drove my dad's old '49 Chevy, which my friends named the rat trap because of the upholstery that was hanging down.

Many girls liked making the rounds with their boyfriends in their upscale cars, and I didn't have much to offer in that respect. When I pressured my dad into buying a new vehicle, he would say, "Well, you will at least know that a girl is not dating you for your money." I'll have to admit that I did have a fascination and admiration for those beautiful machines that travelled past Lewis' Drive-in, the Clock, Ma Crate's and other places around Greer.

After a Friday night Greer High football game, it was customary to drive through town honking the horn in celebration, as it was the event of the week.

The cars shined from the waxed effort put forth, with their half-moon or flipper hubcaps, rolled and pleated upholstery and dual exhausts with chrome extensions from their glass-pack mufflers. Some had cut-offs, that you could switch off and on, from the car's interior.

Some hot rodders, like Jerry Tuck, would customize their vehicles, as he did with his 1949 Mercury. Others, like Bunchy Godfrey, would trade for a new convertible each year.

I remember going with old friend Ronnie Strange to race someone at 1 a.m. on a deserted country road. Ronnie ripped a transmission in his car, and we went to his grandfather's garage, and he replaced it before sunrise. It was not by coincidence that he later owned a huge junkyard in Greer. The guy knew his cars. People from out of town would show up to challenge Norman Peace, in the white '55 Chevy that he drove around town.

Jimmy Benson was another young guy who sported some great-looking rides, and he began hauling vehicles from up north and selling them. He went on to become a financial success with his dealerships, which are scattered around the upstate.

At his dealership in Greer, he has a duplication of the inside of Lewis' Drive-in, with the counter, its stools, tables and even a jukebox, which has many of the hits of the '50s. All inside of a showroom for his classic, beautifully refurbished cars, which dazzled me upon inspection.

Jimmy is a charitable man, who gives back, in so many ways, to his community. As a self-made man he found financial success, starting out small and building his car business, year by year. In the 1950s, he was truly a member of the hot-rod set.

New and Old Sounds in Music

Greer reflected changes made nationwide in America, embracing the hotrod craze, with places like Bakersfield, Ca. establishing new trends, as well as the new on the scene Rock-and-Roll music, which I listened to on my favorite jukebox at Bruce's Lunch.

The 1950s had music for all occasions. There were beautiful hymns that we sang in church and that the Blue Ridge Quartet sang over the radio in our home. There was also music to love to and cry by after the breakup like "It's All in the Game" by Tommy Edwards. There was music to slow dance to like "Smoke Gets in your Eyes" by the Platters, or to shag (dance) to like Billy Ward and the Dominoes' "Sixty Minute Man," or other beach music songs.

As the 1950s progressed, the swing music was not as popular, country music and Blue Grass still thrived, but was being rivalled by the new Rock-and-Roll sound. Rhythm and blues stayed popular, with artists like Clyde McPhatter and the Drifters, Laverne Baker, Joe Turner, and Ruth Brown, all of whom recorded on the Atlantic label. Talent has a way of finding an opening to success.

The blues and jazz were still popular. I lost sleep listening to B.B. King on a Memphis radio station late at night. I followed his career through the years and attended his concerts whenever I could, because I dearly loved to hear him pick his guitar, that he named Lucille.

Up to the mid '50s we couldn't listen to black artists on the white radio station, but we did attend their concerts. We were also able to hear them on jukeboxes around town. Their success did encourage new recording companies, like Motown.

The first big Rock-and-Roll hit "Rock Around the Clock" by Bill Haley and the Comets seemed to encourage others. Buddy Holly achieved stardom backed up by his group, the Crickets. He accepted an ill-advised invitation to fly to the next destination on his tour, and he died in a plane crash with two other performers, Richie Valens and Jiles Perry Richardson, Jr., aka, the Big Bopper.

And then there was doo-wop. I fell in love with it because I loved harmony, and I was fascinated by the backups just as much as I was by lead singers. Groups like the Skyliners, with lead singer Jimmy Beaumont, and the beautiful high voice of Janet Vogel; Dion and the Belmonts; and the Flamingoes with perhaps the best smooching song of the decade, "I Only Have Eyes for You."

A young man from Tupelo, Mississippi, by the name of Elvis Presley, moved rock and roll to the top. His black, wavy hair, good-looking features, and pelvic thrusts as he sang, drove some of the younger female population wild. Waters Record Shop on Randall Street in Greer was where I bought my first record, and they stayed busy in those years. Greer was lively in the 1950s and early 1960s. Communication and new lifestyles accelerated and featured great social change throughout America, which, through the popularization of TV and Hollywood, all trickled down to Greer.

ANNIE, AN INCONSPICUOUS STAR

There are those who blossom late, the cream on the bottom that floats to the top, the one who prefers to go unnoticed, hanging in the shadow, allowing others to hog the spotlight. In her own shy way, that was, and still is, Ann Wilson White-Butler.

Annie wasn't alone in having her talents hidden, mainly because she, along with others, wasn't given the chance to compete. If one wasn't tall, then she was already at a disadvantage on a basketball court. There was no girls' tennis, track, golf, or cross-country team at Greer High, not even a softball team.

Then what was a girl to do in the Greer of the 1950s and early sixties? There were intramural sports, where one could at least learn the rules of volleyball in the fall, basketball during the winter, then softball in the spring. The decision for such opportunities ultimately rested in the hands of Greenville County Schools and monetary decisions that were made placed girls sports near the bottom of the priority list. Sports, in general, were near the bottom because the varsity football program would only allow around 35 players to participate.

There was the notion, held by some, that girls did not need athletics, like guys. Time spent learning to sew, cook and how to become a lady was more beneficial, in preparing one for life. Joining the Junior Cotillion might be appropriate for some but not for Annie.

Annie Wilson took the business school route after high school, and eventually wound up working for the *Louis & Nashville Railroad* in their IBM department.

She relocated to Jacksonville, Fla. with CSX and retired after 33 years, finding during that time many athletic endeavors in which to participate, such as playing tennis, bowling, beach volleyball, golf and especially running.

She began to run and work out at gyms in the afternoon. She married her true love, in fact, on a sand volleyball court. She became the athlete she wasn't allowed to become in her youth. Some of her accomplishments are as follows:

> In 1978 she won her first tennis singles title in Louisville, Kentucky.

1982-1985 She ran on a five-woman racing team for "Athletic Attics Sports."

> In 1983 she ran her first marathon, which she finished in less than four hours.

1988-1999 She was named Captain of the CSX Ladies Tennis Team.

1992-1998 She was named President of the Jacksonville Volleyball Club.

In 1997 she and her partner won second place in the Florida State Beach Doubles Volleyball Championship, held in Miami, Fla.

In 2006 she won the "Ladies Club Championship" in a golf club where she plays.

Annie has trouble finding space for the trophies she has won, in various sports. *The Jacksonville Times* honored her, in an article entitled "Annie White…Queen of All Sports", a fitting tribute to a deserving lady.

Like many of us, Annie has had to pay for all that activity in several sports, having had both knees replaced and a reverse shoulder replacement, along with a few other ailments. She is now back at it again. Something tells me that she is not ready for the sewing circle, just yet.

From a mill village guy from Victor to a shy girl from Apalache, it warms my heart to see her live her dreams. She is one of a kind and a model for all of us. Run, Annie, run!!

THE UNFORGETTABLE, UNCOMPROMISING, CREATIVE, AND ADVENTUROUS BILL GROCE

There are many adjectives and images that spring forth after a life-long association with the man who affected many with his persuasiveness and unpredictability. Life was interesting with him around, from childhood on.

My first encounter with Bill was outside of Davenport Junior High during the early 1950s. He was engaged in a bare-knuckle contest with someone, and Bill was not doing so well until he landed one on his opponent below the belt, and from that point forward Bill made short work of him. I stored away that knowledge in case I became an adversary. Fortunately, we became good friends.

As teenagers, a group of boys, me included, would gather in woods some referred to as the scout property, located by U.S. Highway 29, aka Wade Hampton Boulevard or the Super

Highway, which was the first highway to have four lanes in our area.

We spent some summer days and nights camping, cooking a large pot of beans of different varieties in an old black pot, telling jokes, lies, passing gas, and playing games. It was an inexpensive vacation, as few of us had sufficient funds to head out of town. Occasionally, Bill would create entertainment with his eureka moments that we came to expect, and they never included careful planning.

No venture, or so it seemed in the day, was worth the time spent unless some degree of risk manifested itself. So off we went one summer night, when Bill decided that we should go skinny-dipping at Suttles Swimming Pool, which was closed at the time.

The pool was located a short distance away across Wade Hampton Boulevard, and we had no emergency escape plan in place, in case we were caught. In the words of Robert Burns, *the best laid schemes o' mice an' men gang aft agley* (often go astray) ring true to this day. Since the front entrance to the pool was not deemed to be an intelligent choice, we climbed the fence that surrounded it.

Several of us removed our clothing outside of the fence, since we thought a quick escape might be necessary, and climbing a fence while carrying our garments might prove difficult.

I won't give the identities of others involved in this adventure, for fear of placing them in an unfavorable situation with wives, employers, and relatives. Oh, what the hell! Why should

I accept the blame for everything? There were my old friends, Mack Allen, Truman Tillotson, Freddie Roland, Dan Howard, Carol Williams, Pat Sudduth, Alton Bell, Billy Allen, Leland Campbell, Billy Smith, Neal Dacus and a couple of others, whom I can't recall.

We agreed that this operation would require a certain amount of cooperation by all in keeping noise to a minimum to avoid being discovered. It was with wide-eyed anticipation of a quick response from the pool's security, be it the owners or someone whom they had hired, that dire consequences were expected when Bill decided to liven the night with a cannonball off the pool's diving board, accompanied by a good Southern *Yeehaw!* The lights came on and we were scrambling to our nearest exit.

Dan Howard and I put our clothes on in the grass median of the Super Highway after having carefully straddled the fence in our "each man for himself" escape, as we scattered in many directions. We made the local news around Greer, since there was not very much excitement in our small community in those days. Overheard in a beauty parlor by the mom of one of our cast the next day went something like this: *I tell you, Mabel, there wuz two boys, standing naked, in the middle of the Super Highway. What is this world coming to?*

The police had to have been amused as well. Dan Howard and I were seen climbing down in a ravine beside the highway, hidden away behind some bushes when we heard a policeman's words telling us to come out. I heard one chuckle when I replied: "There's no one down here!"

Eventually I ran alone across the property where Jimmy Benson's car dealership is located, which was then an open field, when suddenly I felt nothing but air under my feet. One foot touched a dirt bank as I descended, and my next stop was face-down on the pavement of a nearby road, with the loud blast from the horn of a truck informing me of my hazardous location. As I attempted to recover the breath that had escaped my body, I continued my trek toward the scout property and the woods, where we were camping.

It was upon entering the woods that I considered the fact that one in our midst may have been caught by policemen and escorted back to our camping headquarters to wait for the rest. It was with that thought in mind that I moved through the woods with as little noise as possible when, suddenly, a spotlight appeared, and I frantically began running. I then heard the undisguised laugh of Bill, who said "You thought I was a cop, didn't you?"

We didn't have cell phones then. Only a few of us had a phone in our homes and those had at least two other parties sharing the line. Few of us had TVs, microwaves didn't exist, and there were many other conveniences that are present today that weren't around then. We had each other and created our own entertainment. Our pockets were, for the most part, empty, but we created some memories and cemented some friendships on those slow summer days of the 1950s. Bill was to create more adventures in my life.

Frog Gigging with Bill Groce

Lewis' Drive-in, the Clock, and Ma Crates were all popular drive-in restaurants in Greer, and gathering places for young people in the 1950s and '60s.

After attending a Sunday-night church service, I was sitting in my car with Pat Sudduth at the Clock Drive-in when Bill Groce drove up and suggested that we go frog gigging.

"Do I look like I'm dressed to go frog gigging?" I asked. Bill then applied his usual ploy of reducing one's manhood, as he began to refer to me in a feminine manner which sometimes worked in convincing others to join his activities. The three of us were off to frog gig, with me dressed in a sport coat and tie. To Greer Lake, we travelled.

"I have a boat we can use," explained Bill, as we drove along in his Studebaker, which held everything a person could possibly need to survive in its trunk in case a nuclear holocaust should occur. I was expecting him to pull a boat from his trunk when we arrived. I found him, instead, beating the lock from a chain, which was wrapped around a tree. Attached to the chain was a rowboat.

"Bill, is this your boat?" I asked. "No," he replied, "but I'm certain that it has been here long enough to be considered abandoned, and should rightfully belong to the person who claims it." No attempts on our part to alter his thinking on the subject convinced Bill, as he soon had the boat in the water.

Bill Groce's version of gigging frogs didn't involve a gig at all, but a .22 caliber rifle and a strong light, as we soon harvested enough frog legs with the firearm to cook for breakfast the next morning. After a couple of trips around the lake, Bill decided that he hated to see the boat go to waste and that it should be moved to the home of his friend Bill Smith's grandfather.

He was convinced, despite our objections, that we could transport the boat on top of his car. I gave up trying to talk him out of something once his mind was made up. We steadied the boat on top of the Studebaker, with the vessel measuring longer than the car, as Bill, with all four windows rolled down, wrapped a strong cable around the boat and through the windows, time and again, until he was certain that the boat was secured to the vehicle.

I was the designated driver, as Bill chose to sit on the fender of the Studebaker, like the captain of a ship, holding the chain that was attached to the boat. I drove slowly, carefully navigating the backroads to Wade Hampton Boulevard, at which point we encountered a problem when two Greer policemen, patrolling in the opposite direction, saw our peculiar looking vehicle. A siren and flashing light soon followed, and after we stopped, both policemen approached us scratching and shaking their heads.

"What have you boys been up to?" asked one policeman. Unable to think of an appropriate response to the question, I responded by telling the truth, that we had been frog gigging. "In a sport coat and tie?" he asked. I then explained that it was a "spur of the moment" decision and that we had decided to move the boat to a friend's house, located just a short distance up U.S. Highway 29.

The policeman who was the designated spokesman asked if we realized that we were breaking the law by transporting a boat in this manner and that it was also illegal to ride on a fender. Pat and I finally convinced both policemen to allow us to drive the short distance up Highway 29, as he uttered a final comment: "Alright, boys, we're gonna let you off, this time, but get off the highway. Danged if this doesn't look like something from outer space."

I wasn't around for the official christening of Bill's next venture, but I understand that it took place at the home of Bill Smith's grandfather, after Bill had decided that the boat was so large that it could be sawed in half, to make two boats. If you're wondering how that turned out, both halves sank.

The Mysterious Explosion on Burgess Hill

We were camping at the scout property when Bill Groce revealed the fact that Tom "Flip" Singleton and some other guys were camping on Burgess Hill not far away. Proposing that we should go raid them in the middle of the night, we all climbed on board, thinking it would be an innocent and fun activity.

As we approached their camping site, quietly and cautiously, we eventually witnessed the fire they had built on top of the hill amid a grove of hardwood trees.

We decided beforehand to toss pebbles in the top of the trees, and we threw them at intervals, to arouse their curiosity in determining the source of the sound. We heard comments such as, "What was that?" as they looked up into the trees. Suddenly, the ground shook from a large explosion that caused limbs to tumble from the tops of the trees. The exit from the grove of trees was swift, as the guys ran in many directions, with our group included.

No one had expected Bill Groce to deliver his oversized, homemade firecracker, which, even he admitted, was a bit stronger than he had intended. Fortunately, there were no injuries. I'm thankful that we all were able to survive Bill's many experiments.

Bill had a strong interest in science, especially chemistry, and later, after he finished Newberry College, where he played football, alongside my friend Dennis Lynn, and majored in science, he eventually owned his own chemical company and worked for a while in the bomb plant near Aiken, S.C. The news of the mysterious explosion on Burgess Hills lingered for a long time and it did provide some interesting discussion among the residents of Greer.

Spelunking? What's that?

It was after I had finished at the University of Georgia and was teaching at Central Elementary in Woodruff, S.C., that Bill Groce called me and asked if I would like to go spelunking with him. When he explained that it was cave exploring, I pictured a storybook cave, the type one might see in a Jules Verne movie.

Bill educated me, somewhat, as we ventured toward Trenton, Ga., in the northwest corner of the state, close to Alabama. Cloudland Canyon had several caves, and they were not the kind of "walk-into" type of caves that you might see in a movie.

Bill did mention some necessary items associated with spelunking. We would need lights, and batteries, as well as rope, food, and a supply of water. We would also need to sign in at the mouth of the cave, so a ranger, who checked the list to find out who entered and exited the cave, would have knowledge of that fact. If a party entered and failed to exit, then they were presumed lost.

Caves have tributaries, which have other feeders and forks that branch off from those. Arrows were drawn inside of the caves, revealing the direction one should travel, as well as the way to exit. The rule was to never venture into the unexplored parts of a cave. Follow the arrows. No light is present in those catacombs, which are limestone formations, and the temperature remains the same all year long. The entrance to our chosen cavern to explore was small. My debut into spelunking was a hair-raising, wide-eyed, heart-pounding experience.

I entered the cave headfirst, crawling through a small opening, with flashlight on, when suddenly I began sliding, in total darkness, down a slick incline, without knowing where my skid would end. *Would it be against a wall? Would it be over an edge, down to the next level? If so, how far would I fall?* The slide was about 60-70 feet into the cave, but it seemed to last forever and was accompanied by my screams.

"Are you OK?" asked Bill, with a laugh that could be singled out from a million others.

"Hell, no!" I answered back. After he found me, he asked me to turn my light off and sit there for a minute. After a while, my racing heart was beating normally, and we continued our exploration.

Caves can expose phobias and one of Bill's, a well-kept secret, was revealed. We came upon a chimney, a narrow passageway into another part of the cave. Bill explained that he would go through first, since he was larger and in case he might not fit through the opening. If I went first, then I would be trapped inside, if he became stuck. I, therefore, went last going in, and first, coming out. He had been lodged into such an opening before, not able to crawl out and was forced to rip off a jacket he was wearing to dislodge himself.

Bill's breathing became more pronounced, and when I inquired about it, he explained that he was claustrophobic. I don't ever remember Bill being afraid of anything, even after sleeping on top of a water tower.

We secured a rope, which we used to repel down to another level, and that wasn't a problem, because we both had experienced mountain climbing and repelling in the Marines. We would later use the rope to climb up, as we exited the cave.

We were walking along a ledge in the cave when I asked Bill how deep the abyss below might be. He dropped a coin, and it kept falling, on its long descent downward. Suddenly, the ledge on which we were inching along, ran out.

"Bill," I asked, "What do we do now?" Bill fell forward, placing his hands on the other wall of the narrow tunnel we were inching through, which faced the one where we had been walking. He then placed the soles of his feet on the opposite wall, where we were standing. He walked it, wedged between the two walls and facing straight down, for about five yards.

"No way!" I exclaimed. At that point I was determined to go back, but finally he walked me through it, after a lengthy conversation, convincing me of the safety of the climb. It wasn't as hair-raising as I expected and not nearly as bad on the return.

The trip to the middle of the underground chamber was worth the risk. We entered a huge room in the cave, which was about 200 yards long and 100 yards high.

A stream flowed through the room, where native rainbow trout swam. There was a waterfall, accented by quartz crystals, which glowed and sparkled, as the beams of our lights reflected on them. All of this with the stalactites, icicle-like formations, hanging from the roof, and stalagmites, of similar construction and protruding from the floor, located approximately 2.5 miles from the entrance, really did make it seem like a journey into another world.

What an adventure! How much living we packed into such a short period of time. Sitting around a campfire, once we exited the cave, might have been the best adventure of all, as we talked for hours. Bill reveled in our venture. We sipped his generic beer, enclosed in a white can, which was labelled "Beer."

While just partially revealing the life of a man who left us so many times with wide eyes, open mouths, and with heads shaking, his saga continues.

There was the incident where he made a new wood floor cleaner for his chemical company, and it cleaned the floor so well that it just kept on cleaning to the bottom. He wound up buying a customer a new floor.

I drove down to see him at his place of business once and I was greeted by a horde of dogs of many colors. Bill didn't have any Easter chickens to dye, so he decided to color the dogs with a nonpermanent substance. He loved his dogs and was prone to adopt strays and keep them at his business.

He went diving in the water around the battery in Charleston and collected a few Civil War relics and used a vacuum system on the bottom of the Chestatee River in Georgia, to obtain gold dust. He also gave me a shark's tooth, one of several that he found below Columbia, where the ocean at one time was that far inland. He had the teeth verified by an archeologist at the University of South Carolina, who said that the great white shark that the teeth came from could have held eleven people in its mouth.

The unpredictability of Bill Groce made life interesting for us all, and we kept a watchful eye out, due to his unannounced, spontaneous actions. How he managed to talk a sweet, pretty girl like Mary Ellen (Mish) Reese to marry him might have been the biggest mystery of all, but, as I said, he was very persuasive. Bill became a scout leader and shared his knowledge of the outdoors with young people, and one of my nephews, Jeff Wood, was one of the recipients.

I visited my old friend in a home in Augusta, Ga., where he was suffering from a stroke, accompanied by some dementia. I fed him some madeleine cookies that I had baked. He told me that his short-term memory was gone but that he remembered all our time together. We laughed and recalled them, and I left him on a sad note, wanting to help him escape from his jail and relive our adventures. He seemed so out of place there. He passed away a few weeks later.

I miss my old friend but the time I spent with Bill was filled with excitement and adventure. We packed a lot of living into a brief amount of life. If living each day to its fullest is what counts most on this earth, then Bill died a rich man and I'm even richer, for having had his presence in my life.

THE NEARLY LOST ART OF HITCHHIKING

What once was a method we relied upon to travel is now near extinction. Occasionally, I see some guy standing by the road with his thumb extended, praying that this will be the vehicle that will give him a ride, only to be disappointed.

My dad in the 1940s and '50s, usually picked up hitchhikers. In fact, I heard one of my uncles tell other relatives, while we were sitting on the front porch, that Dad would not only pick up a hitchhiker, but would go 10 miles out of his way to take him home. They really made me angry because I knew they were poking fun at him, and Dad would smile and tell me that it was alright. I didn't want anyone using him as the object of a joke.

The remark made by my uncle was true and was a testament to my dad's character. Our financial assets didn't add up to much, but we, as a family, were always willing to share. It was a practice that was passed on by my parents to their children. As a result, just like my father, I picked up hitchhikers as well, but, perhaps unlike him, never with complete confidence. I also spent time beside a highway with my thumb out.

One young man that I allowed to ride with me asked, as we travelled down the road, if I wasn't a little wary of picking up strangers, and I replied that I wasn't, if I had my Smith and Wesson pistol with me. His eyes widened a little, but I never smiled. I didn't tell him that I wasn't really carrying a firearm. There really was a risk, I would guess, but one that I was willing to take because I knew how difficult it was to catch a ride.

People were reluctant to pick up strangers, and if you wanted success in hitching a ride, then there were unwritten rules you should observe. Personal appearance was important, so a well-groomed person had better results than one who wasn't. A big smile also helped. Roadside appearance was very important.

Two people thumbing together also had a harder task in catching a ride because a driver might not trust having one passenger sitting behind him. I personally would never pick up two or more people for that reason unless they happened to be in the armed services. I also would not pick up a person if I had another family member with me.

People hitchhiked for a variety of reasons. In the case of Pat Sudduth and Walter Burch, neither had vehicles of their own, so they had to find a ride back to Presbyterian College in Clinton, S.C., following a weekend at home. If they couldn't find a ride, then they had to thumb (hitchhike). The parents had given instructions to stay at school or find a ride back in advance. Many college students hitched a ride in those days.

Doyle Loftis and Darius Loftis talked me into taking a trip to North Myrtle Beach with them. We were to drive for a lady and her daughter. She would provide a place for us to stay and meals. When we arrived at her beach cottage, she asked, "Where are you guys staying?" We were forced to pool our resources to pay for a small room, an unexpected expense. She was nice enough to invite us for a couple of meals.

It was a short beach trip, as I had limited money, and I was soon on the highway, alone, attempting to find transportation back to Greer. After no success hitchhiking, I walked into a truck stop for a Coke, talked to a driver at the food counter, who asked where I was from, and he just happened to be going to Greenville. He actually gave me a ride to Taylors, and I walked from there to my home. Such luck was rare.

Don Wall and I bravely began a hitchhiking trip to the coast but after being stuck in Union all night, we decided to turn around and hitch a ride back to Greer.

The dark side of hitchhiking was revealed as Stanley Godfrey and I, with 25 dollars between us and a yearning for salt air, decided to brave a trip hitchhiking. We were off to a good start after hitching a ride to Columbia. After being picked up on U.S. Highway 76/378, we were making progress until our ride informed us that he was turning onto a secondary road.

Stanley and I found ourselves stuck in the middle of a swamp on a dark, moonless night. We had to play games to stay awake, as it was well past midnight, and we were on watch for an alligator strolling out of the swamp for a snack. An Opel Kadett went past, applied the brakes as if the driver might give us a ride, then continued on.

We finally caught a ride with a man in a 1949 Mercury. Stanley yelled "Shotgun!" as we sprinted toward the vehicle. I really didn't care, as I would have the back seat to myself. Stanley was seated beside the driver and discovered that there was no windshield on his side. He was shivering very quickly. We never asked the driver how he lost part of his windshield.

The driver exhibited odd behavior as we drove down the road. He never smiled and he would turn towards Stanley, who had already turned blue from the early morning air that was blowing, and gaze, without speaking. He repeated his looks several times, with a glance toward me through the rearview mirror occasionally, as we continued down the road. Stan finally looked in my direction and communicated with his eyes, which I'm positive meant, "Be ready to run like hell."

The term *serial killer* wasn't used much in those days, but I definitely would have considered him a suspect after my imagination went to work. Who knows? The guy could have been a Sunday school teacher. He let us out in Conway, S.C. We thanked him and he smiled for the first time. I was just glad he didn't pull out a machete and start hacking.

When we reached Highway 17, near Ocean Drive, we saw a couple of Greer High friends, Michael Clayton and Joe Brunson, whose car was beside the road with no gas. We pushed their car to a nearby service station and drained what little excess gas there was out of the pumps and into the car's tank, since the station was not open.

When we told them of our experience in the swamp, a surprised look came across their faces. They had seen a couple of guys hitchhiking in a swampy section of the highway, and Michael had said that one of those guys looked like Bowman and they slowed down. Then both said "Nah! Bowman wouldn't be out in the middle of a swamp, thumbing." They then continued on.

There was a time when families had one vehicle if they were lucky. If you wanted one for yourself, then you worked, saved money, and purchased what you could afford. Your other options were to depend upon a friend for a ride, call a taxi, ride a train or bus, or stand beside the road with your thumb out. Lots of memories about the nearly lost art of hitchhiking. Be careful out there.

WHAT I LEFT BEHIND

What do I miss most from those days in the 1940s and 1950s and what would I have tossed in the trash bin? The P.F. Flyers that I wore were pretty good, for the money, but I always had the feeling that I could have wound up in a ditch, due to a blowout, if I ran too fast. The ASICs that I wear today are a vast improvement.

I miss sitting on Pappy Burns' porch, in Cross Hill, listening to his tales. It would have made me happy if all my students could have attended one of his sessions. I also love hymns of that era, like "Whispering Hope," splashing in streams, losing track of time, and skinny-dipping under a waterfall, even though I'd probably scare the fish if they had to look at me now.

The freshly varnished floors of the past have become synthetic in many gyms today. I enjoyed, and still do, the vibration of a basketball striking the wooden floors and the crack of a wooden bat in what was once referred to as the ballpark. I especially enjoyed watching Robert Lynn hit a ball one night at a Greer American Legion game. It went over the lights in rightfield, and I think they found the ball somewhere around Simpsonville.

I played baseball and tackle football, at times, with guys from Sunnyside, Slabtown, and Green Town, all black communities in Greer. I would run into Willy Dodd and another guy nicknamed "Red China," uptown, and we would trash-talk about who could play ball better. They would put together a team and we'd do the same, then play at Victor Ballpark on Saturdays. One team or the other would win, but the worst thing that would happen would be a little name-calling, like "soda cracker" or "chocolate drop." The "N" word was never used. The loser was always invited back to try again.

It was easy to see the talent out there, and, in a segregated world, those guys were never allowed to come into the YMCA and play basketball. That always bothered me because you're never a champion until you take on all competition. They deserved that chance to compete.

I miss sitting around a table with my family, sharing made from scratch food and having conversation with one another, the smell of our kitchen when Mother baked her cakes and pies, and the potato pancakes she made from those leftover mashed spuds.

I inherited from my mother the love of flowers, especially the wild ones, such as the morning glory, the mountain daisy, and wild roses. I've searched, diligently, for the Cherokee rose, with no success.

What did I learn? Being raised with three sisters, I learned that it is wise to be kind to women, as it is also not always important to win an argument. Playing the game hard, fair and by the rules is more important than winning, but it is a hell of a lot more fun to come out on top. Working out algebra equations was not fun, but it did make me think more, and the brain does need exercise. I know less about women than I did at birth.

Eventually, I found that freckles are not so bad. In fact, I referred to one of the prettiest girls I've ever known as "my speckled beauty."

I treasure, still, my visits to Rosie's, with Michele and the girls, listening to the liars spin their tales about the old days. The best hotdog in town is another reason to visit. When I'm there, sometimes I'll ride down to Virginia Avenue, to the old ball field. I can still hear Hal Huey's voice when I went to bat, "Ducks on the pond, lefty, ducks on the pond."

I love the memories of sleeping on Windy Hill Beach, awakening to the sound of seagulls, watching a girl with Shirley MacLain eyes, with a figure like Marilyn Monroe, strolling through the surf where the beaches were thinly populated in the days before the sea oats and dunes were replaced by condominiums. Shagging and drinking Falstaff at the Pad in Ocean Drive was also fun.

Then there were the people I met along the way, my heroes, and heroines, who were life changing. Mine came by accident, or so it seemed, until I considered the fact that, maybe, God intervened and decided that I needed help, after straying off track. I'm still feeding my redbirds, out back, and occasionally one cocks his head to the side, and looks at me, as if to ask, "Are you staying straight?"

I am the only one of my immediate family still alive, but some great memories remain. The cohesiveness and love among us became so strong that it will always be a part of me.

I have never chosen to use the statement, like some, that "I wouldn't change a thing." There were some decisions I made that were wrong, and if I had a chance to change them, I would, even if it meant rearranging my life. As for the journey with my family, it was the greatest part of growing up.

I can still feel the breeze blowing through the hardwoods on Teague Road, not too far from Mountville, in Laurens County, watching the swaying, back and forth, of the golden oat field that is about ready for harvesting. If I had to choose a launching pad to the hereafter, because of the peacefulness and beauty of this setting, it would be there, lying on my back, in the middle of the field, with the spirits of Buck, Bozo, Nero, and the rest of my animals by my side cheering me on, with background music, of course. I'm still a boy, at heart, who never grew up.